BALANCE FOR Busy Moms

A Stress-free Guide to **Tranquility**

COMPILED BY
HEATHER EDEN

D0875125

CM Publisher
c/o Marketing for Coach, Ltd
Second Floor
6th London Street
W2 1HR London (UK)

www.cm-publisher.com
info@cm-publisher.com

ISBN: 978-0-9575561-9-5

Published in UK, Europe, US and Canada

Book Cover and Inside Layout: Alvaro Beleza

Table of Contents

Foreword

By Heather Elif Pilon

We've done it. We've all crossed that threshold into the adventures of motherhood. We've seen our hearts expand beyond our imagination and our skinny jeans get consigned to the backs of our closets. Daily, we do our best to take care of our children, take care of our duties at work, and find what time we can for ourselves. However, at times, fulfilling our responsibilities for our family can be daunting. There's so much to do and seemingly so little time; we want to do anything and everything for our children, but what about Mama?

Whatever stage of Motherhood you may be in, **Balance for Busy Moms** is a fantastic source of encouragement, anecdotal support, and down-to-earth, Mom-to-Mom advice. Each co-author conveys their story, their expertise, and their quest for self-improvement. The topics include such things as self-care, yoga, cleansing, organizing your home, slowing down for some meditation, and gracefully making your way into grand-motherhood. The chapters touch the hearts of mothers and ask us to slow down and surrender. Not in the raising-the-white flag and giving up type of way. Rather, in a way that encourages moms to take a collective inhalation and feel acceptance of where we are at this very moment, and move forward from there.

Heather Love Eden worked tirelessly to find authors who could bring a sense of calm and peace into the hearts of every Mother who reads these pages. In addition to being a mother of two, Heather is a dancer, a photographer, writer, and holistic health and lifestyle coach. I first met Heather in 2006, during her globe-trotting days, while we were both living and working in South Korea. My fondest memory of our time together was staying at her home in Busan one fall weekend, when we had a chance to share our life stories while walking along the beach. One thing that struck me was Heather's determination to persevere, no matter how daunting the challenges that were facing her. She's never given up her quest for spiritual growth, and *Balance for Busy Moms* is one example of her heartfelt determination to connect Mothers with each other around the globe.

– Heather Elif Pilon

Hongik University Professor and Yoga Instructor
Mother of Two
Seoul, South Korea

In Gratitude

Since gratitude is a noun, I'd like to give it to the reader. Gratitude is nothing we can see, but we can carry it, feel it, give it, receive it, create it, and enjoy it. It clears our energy palettes. It sends light to our hearts. It is the springboard from which love emerges. I'm giving you gratitude because if I hadn't seen myself in every mom, every day, rushing around, talking to their babies, protecting their babies and children, in their workout suits, sweats, hair tied in a bun, no makeup, full of worries, full of curiosity, full of love, in need to slow down, in need to make more time for themselves, in need to love and forgive more, in trouble, undecided, unfulfilled, ready for a real conversation, ready for authentic connection, with a desire to life in purpose, with an open heart, with guilt, with tension, with big dreams, on the fence, off course, on course, ready to act, afraid to move, lost for words, carefree, clueless, and searching for freedom, I wouldn't have worked harder to fill in the gaps, let go, heal, forgive, and love in order to serve other moms. The *Book of Miracles* says that "Jesus calls us similarly: Choose me as your teacher and let me teach you that your life is a classroom, that you may learn to embrace the circumstances of your life in gratitude. Come to me and accept the lessons that will take you home on the wings of forgiveness, with the song of love in your heart." (*The Book of Miracles*). So let us find our wings together, for my dream has always been to fly with others.

I would like to give a huge thanks to my publisher, Christine Marmoy, for being such an amazing mentor, friend, and business coach. When I said "*Balance for Busy Moms,*" and explained to her what was going on in my life, and how much I love this vision and how much I want to make time to get this project started, she said, "It sounds like you need a stress-free guide to tranquility." We laughed, and I knew right then this book was going to have a big impact on the lives of moms everywhere. She has taught me the true meaning of collaboration and teamwork. I will always be grateful to her for the opportunity to get this powerful message out to the world, for moms.

I also want to give a very special thanks to all the twenty-nine co-authors who worked so hard with me to make this book the most amazing stress-free guide for all moms of this time. Many of the co-authors are fellow graduates of IIN; some are life coaches, business coaches, mamapreneurs, spiritual coaches, artists, and writers who fell in love with the vision and answered the call to serve. Most of them are moms, and all are lovers of life. Every chapter is a pouring of their hearts with conviction to live in their own truth as they define what they do in service to share with others. They are the most amazing group of women I have ever met, and I will always consider us the *Balance for Busy Moms* tribe.

I also want to give thanks to my mom, Carol Pearson, in remembrance of her life (1949-2004). She was a very spiritual person, who learned how to love through parenting my brother and me. She introduced me to juicing in 1998 and sent me to Alaska after college so I could explore God's country and find the strength I needed to endure life. She always supported me when I made decisions for big change. Thank you, Mom, and I love you.

Introduction

Tranquility is that beautiful, calm feeling of peace without noise, violence, fear, worry, or pain. It's merely impossible to attain from the outside world. It is, however, possible to reach a state of inner tranquility. Moms have the greatest task of balancing the most demanding and challenging jobs on the planet with grace and poise. Feelings can change in a matter of seconds, from great joy to utter frustration. Shifts occur daily in our schedules, forcing us to become flexible, adaptable, and corporative. Our children are our biggest priorities as they grow and their needs change. Self-pleasure decreases as the demand for accommodation and responsibility calls. We find ourselves hidden in the vast busyness, as time moves perpetually through the years, while we continue to give. Motherhood is triumphing and wearisome all in one. Stress is the enemy, and as if we need more to worry about, there are broken systems to weed through and stand against. Where is the relief? How do we win? How can we be certain that everything will be OK?

I've asked myself, "Would I be a mother if I knew what I know right now?" The answer is *yes*. I would, because I can, and my purpose on this planet is to evolve. No matter how difficult the circumstances, moms have a natural inner strength of protection and endurance. Raising children is our great duty. Sometimes we need help from outside sources. "It takes a village to raise a child" is a common statement that comes to mind (Anonymous Proverb). Well, I say, it takes a village to help a mom raise a child. Moms go to churches; moms go to meet ups; moms go to school; moms go to lengthy journeys to help them parent properly. What is the key? How do some families raise healthy, emotionally stable, independent kids who become happy and successful as adults? While others raise children who turn out the opposite on the spectrum? Let's look at the parents. Every parent I know, with kids who are thriving, have one value in common—Self-

Respect. Self-care has got to be the most important principle a mom learns to practice on a daily basis. Without daily self-care practices, Mom is not fully able to care for others, including her children.

By God's grace, I have found a village to help Mom, and this is my reason: In my experience, being a mom on the path to freedom and complete wellness has been very isolating and lonely. I don't hide behind religion. I don't hide behind victimization. I don't hide behind excuses. I don't hide behind my past. I am real and on the path to healing, which places me directly in the position for service. Need healing? Love others. Need help? Help others. Need advice? Listen to others. Parenting is an intuitive journey into the heart.

As moms come to realize, one child is completely different from the other. Some things work on one child but have no effect on the next. This is one curious part of our evolution. It is Mom's responsibility to adapt to change and accommodate her children when necessary, and this can weigh heavily on her shoulders—in any circumstance. At the end of the day, we count our blessings. Tomorrow is another day. We have room to grow. The kids will be OK. And each morning, we give thanks for a new day, another chance to love and be loved.

But, what happens when Mom's health is compromised? She is irreplaceable. No one can love her children like she does. No one understands her children like she does. No one knows the heart of her children like she does. Her place in this world is invaluable. No one kisses the way Mom kisses or holds the way she does. Her children need her, and they deeply hold a precious prayer safely inside: "Dear God, please help Mommy so that she can be here with us."

Moms! Of course, accidents happen, and genetics plays a part in illness. There are numerous contributing factors of illness: stress, animal protein, harmful chemicals, environmental pollutants, toxins, negative beliefs, physical trauma, birth defects, fungus, bacteria, and viruses. But can we prevent illness? Good news! Medical scientists have proven that we can prevent illnesses with a clean diet, healthy mindset, and healthy lifestyle. This means we can have Heaven on Earth.

Are you with me? When I think of Heaven, I think of tranquility. This book is a compilation of purposeful knowledge for all moms, from prenatal to menopause, single or married, who desire inner tranquility — the quiet core, the relaxed and clear heart chakra. Today's world can be a sensory overload, on top of our busy kids, demanding schedules, and intangible tasks. The idea is to create a calm center, set our daily intentions, and make the magic happen.

I believe you will love this book just as much as I do. I set out to find twenty-nine other certified holistic practitioners, and I found over and beyond what I imagined. I believe we must set the bar and then trust the Universe. You will be amazed. This book was created to help Mom completely transform mind, body, and soul, relative to her own journey, in relation to self-care, foods, diet, lifestyle, healing, parenting, relationships, love, intimacy, self-sustainability, connecting to our planet, art therapy, career, business, dreams, joy, expression, purpose, energy clearing, visualization, simplicity, physical activity, cooking, birth, meditation, and most of all, love. Each chapter is a lesson to assist Mom in every area of her life. Each individual co-author is exceptionally gifted and specializes in her topic. So, make yourself a cup of tea, Mom, and give yourself a moment to enjoy this wonderful stress-free guide to tranquility. You deserve it!

Heather Love Eden

Heather is an International Best-Selling Author, Certified Health and Lifestyle Coach, Speaker, Photographer, and Healing Arts Abstract Painter.

Heather has a BA in Creative Writing from LSU and a Certification in Health Coaching from IIN. She is the founder of Complete Wellness Coaching, and the *Balance for Busy Moms* Tribe Heather Eden coaches from the Complete Wellness philosophy of fulfilling twelve areas in life for complete wellness. She also coaches moms and dads on overcoming stress, unhappiness, toxic energy, and unhealthy habits. Complete Wellness means healing mind, body, and spirit through a bio-individual approach, where diet and lifestyle changes become imperative in creating complete positive change.

🏠 www.heathereden.com

🏠 www.balanceforbusymoms.com

f www.facebook.com/completewellnesscoaching

🐦 www.twitter.com/heatherloveeden

ⓟ www.pinterest.com/heatherluveden

in www.linkedin.com/heatherloveeden

LESSON 1

Tranquility in the Kitchen

By Heather Love Eden

~~~

Close your eyes and envision your current kitchen. Are you and your family living with optimum health? Kitchens are wonderful living areas. It's the sacred center of home. If walls could talk, my kitchen would say: good health, joy, functionality, sharing, yummy goodness, creativity, strength, calm, balanced, flow, love. What do your walls say?

In order to have a functionally flowing, healthy kitchen, Mom must bring in the proper food items for her family to eat, learn to prepare and cook healthy foods, keep a clean pantry, toxic-free surfaces, functional appliances, and clean filtered water. Wellness begins when we start trusting our intuitive instincts, and this is important when we work on our health.

DECISION TIME

I am a single mom of two beautiful children. Both births were very hard, emergency C-sections, and their father didn't show up for either. I've had some tough lessons in love, and the experience has brought me to hopelessness several times. However, I have been blessed beyond belief with their lives, and I work hard to take care of us. They have gifted me with the need to honor and cherish myself, and they inspire me along this journey to inner tranquility.

Five years ago, my son kept getting strep throat with very high fevers, which occurred after moving back to the US from South Korea. In Korea, we grew accustomed to eating fairly balanced, home cooked meals. We were rarely sick. Once again, we adjusted to the American culture of eating, and sickness happened often. I found myself with constant sinusitis. Plus, I became overwhelmed with anxiety and depression, and I started taking an anti-depressant medication.

Two years later, I made the decision to change our diet and lifestyle. I wanted a new career in health and wellness. I found IIN, then put myself through school to become a Health Coach, while working fulltime and raising my son.

It was one of the best decisions I made in my life. I was able to live happily without medication and learn new skills to cope with daily stress. A year later, I had a healthy baby girl. Now, I raise my children with more love, and I enjoy a balanced approach to living. My diet and lifestyle changes required me to have an open, flexible, and willing mind to manifest health; and I found home cooking vital for health restoration. It wasn't an easy task, but here is how I did it.

BE A FOOD INVESTIGATOR

Read labels. Here are some ingredients to avoid in food: high fructose corn syrup, sodium nitrate, partially hydrogenated oil of any kind (trans fats), calcium chloride, preservatives, artificial colors or dyes, processed sugar (which reads as sugar), table salt, aspartame, sodium aluminum phosphate, and other ingredients you can't pronounce. I've grown weary of all the toxicity in our food, especially in our fruits and vegetables—waxes, pesticides, insecticides, and the GMO's. Be careful with meat, too. Make sure it is free of antibiotics, sodium nitrate, hormones, fillers, and preservatives.

We want to protect our health and our loved ones' health from becoming a statistic. I buy all organic produce, if possible, at natural food stores and local farmers markets. Learning about farms in your area is fun, and your kids will enjoy it too. Just make sure your local farmers are using nontoxic methods of growing fruits and vegetables.

PANTRY CLEANOUT

Investigate the food in your pantry. Don't be afraid of disposing of foods which contribute to illness. Here are things to remove: expired oils, artificial sweeteners, processed boxed food items with preservatives, canned foods with preservatives, aerosol spray butter and oil, expired condiments, seasonings with MSG, chips with preservatives, crackers with high fructose corn syrup, crackers with partially hydrogenated oils, and anything with processed sugar, bleached flours, and ingredients you cannot pronounce.

COOK TO LIVE

Preparing food is simple once we learn how to eat. I enjoy eating fruit with whole grains, or fruit with granola and almond milk in the morning. I try to stay seasonal with fruits and vegetables. I eat whole grains that digest well in my body, and sometimes I eat gluten-free. Smoothies are awesome in the mornings. They can be super healthy and easy to make.

Grazing trays are fun for lunch and fun for kids: organic no-nitrate turkey slices with mozzarella cheese and baby spinach rolled in a corn tortilla, or dehydrated veggies, avocado slices, and bite-size apples and pears with quick-seared wild tuna (seasoned with Braggs amino acids, turmeric, sea salt, and cracked black pepper). My daughter and I enjoy brown rice with green peas, carrots, chia seeds, and tofu (seared and seasoned with low sodium Tony's, sea salt, and Bragg's amino acids), and a glass of fresh juice—carrots, celery, apple, cucumber.

I prefer vegetable soup with rice or whole wheat noodles, or brown rice for dinner. I cook healthy spaghetti once a week. We also we eat veggies with quinoa and organic no-nitrate turkey, tofu, fish, or roasted red potatoes. I sauté vegetables for 2-5 minutes max, on medium high, in coconut oil (tablespoon), sea salt, cracked pepper, and Braggs Amino Acids (teaspoon). I like baking sweet potatoes with butter, coconut oil, cinnamon, coconut palm sugar, sea salt, and organic cracked black pepper. I also bake turnips, carrots, and apples. They taste great with cinnamon, sea salt, butter, and coconut palm sugar. Baked dishes go well with organic meats and sautéed vegetables, or gluten-free or non-gluten-free pasta dishes.

I use a crockpot to cook beans and vegetables to save time and energy preparing dinner in the winter. I like to soak the peas or beans overnight and rinse them in the morning, then chop vegetables and or organic turkey sausage, and combine everything with seasoning. Let it cook for three hours on high and three hours on low. Boil the water first before adding to the crockpot. Serve with gluten-free pasta or brown rice.

MY 365 DAYS FOOD STAPLES

These super foods are a "must keep stocked" in my kitchen. Over time, I realized the best way to store healthy food supplements is in glass jars. I put medicinal foods in a nearby cabinet away, from heat and for easy access: Chia seeds, flax seeds or grounded seeds, raw cacao nibs or power, walnuts, pecans, sunflower seeds, pumpkin seeds, goji berries, almonds, coconut palm sugar, raw coconut, hemp seeds or power, Brazil nuts, maca powder, coconut oil, and raw honey.

Ideas for foods to keep stocked in your pantry: quinoa, brown rice, whole wheat or gluten-free noodles, an assortment of beans, nuts (some are stored in fridge), whole grain crackers, variety of teas, and essential oils.

Preferred Spices and Condiments: Himalayan pink salt or Celtic sea salt, cinnamon, cumin, curcumin, saffron, black cracked pepper, Bragg's aminos, pure maple syrup, ketchup (no high fructose corn syrup), low sodium Tony's, cayenne pepper, apple cider vinegar, and turmeric.

Ideas for foods to keep stocked in freezer: peas, strawberries, mangos, chopped onions-celery-peppers mixture, kale, and soybeans.

FUNCTIONALITY FABULOUS

These are simple and helpful appliances: blender, juicer, dehydrator, food processor, ceramic cookware, glassware for storage containers and baking, bamboo cutting boards and spoons, stainless steel utensils, a stainless steel or ceramic waffle maker for the kiddos, and most importantly, a high quality water filter (spring water from the ground is the best, rich with necessary minerals. Visit www.findaspring.com for natural spring water).

Also, save money and stay healthy cleaning your kitchen surfaces: mix 1/2 cup water, 1 cup distilled vinegar, and 1/3 lemon juice to a spray bottle. You can also add 2 drops of eucalyptus, lavender, lemon, juniper, pine, thyme, or rosemary essential oils to the solution, and clean happy.

OUR FAVORITES

Our favorite pancake recipe: one cup whole wheat flour, multi-grain or gluten-free pancake mix, 2/3 cup of almond milk (we tend to stay away from dairy), Chia seeds, walnuts, banana, cinnamon, coconut palm sugar, and cacao nibs cooked with coconut oil, topped with butter, and pure maple syrup.

My favorite spaghetti recipe: ground organic turkey—drained, sautéed mushrooms, zucchini, onion, and garlic. Use a blender and mix green bell pepper and carrots with sauce. Combine everything and cook on low for 15 minutes. Add sea salt, cracked red pepper (just a little), black pepper, and turmeric. Serve with whole-wheat noodles or gluten-free noodles.

My daughter's favorite quick dinner: whole grain mild organic cheddar macaroni and cheese with Chia seeds and a side of fresh juice—carrots, celery, apples, and cucumber.

My son's favorite quick dinner: no-nitrate turkey dogs with organic chili beans (seasoned with sea salt, red and black pepper, cayenne, and turmeric), on whole wheat buns, topped with shredded mild natural cheddar cheese, and a side shot of fresh juice—apples, carrots, celery, and cucumber.

My favorite super food smoothie: frozen strawberries, frozen mango, apple, banana, pear, cucumber, carrots, Chia seeds, a scoop of Green Vibrance, and water. I also add cacao nibs, almond butter, hemp seeds, and maca and goji berries for a richer, nutrient-dense consistency and flavor.

Heather Elif Pilon

Heather Elif Pilon has been a yoga practitioner for seventeen years and (finally!) a yoga teacher for the past two years. She's never given up on her spiritual growth. She believes in peaceful parenting, positive affirmations, and the power of love. She allows space for feeling her emotions (the good, the bad, and the ugly) and never holds back on her "happy dance" when the spirit moves her. Heather teaches yoga part-time (both in classes, and privately) in Seoul, where she lives with her husband, Simon, her two boys, Sebastian and Oliver, and their cat, Pasha.

🏠 www.heatherpilon.com

🏠 www.peacefulparent.com

🏠 www.yogaglo.com

LESSON 2

Yoga: Rekindling Your Light

By Heather Elif Pilon

~~~

As many of us have already discovered, carving out some space for physical activity can indeed be a challenge, especially if you have more than one child. For me, getting back to a yoga practice was my goal after the birth of my boys. In this chapter, I hope to tell my story to encourage Moms, both new and experienced, who want to either begin or resume the practice of yoga and challenge that feeling of "not being able to find the time" that arises in us amid the demands of Motherhood.

I feel really grateful to say that I participated in two yoga teacher training courses (TTCs): One in 2008, in Trivandrum, India, and the other in 2009-2011 in Seoul, South Korea (before, during, and a short while after my first pregnancy). The first TTC was at a Sivananda Ashram in Southern India. My second TTC was in South Korea, where we currently live, at a studio called Magic Pond Yoga. By the end of these programs, yoga had become a big part of my life.

Then, in May 2010 and January 2012, my baby boys arrived, twenty months apart. After the first babe, I felt good to be maintaining a light daily yoga practice, including a 10-minute meditation during the baby's naps. The little space I carved out for yoga was giving me time to reset after difficult days and evenings. It also helped release intense, bottled-up emotions resulting from fears of "not doing this right." Even though I was only meditating occasionally, I was still able to find a connection to the personal peace that I had established months before in my yoga studies. In those initial 20 months as a first-time time Mom, I was earnestly delighted and felt as if I were on a path toward the kind of peaceful parenting that had not experienced in my own childhood.

Fast-forward to my second son's arrival, and the trials of Motherhood got ramped up a few hundred notches! The little time for yoga I had with just one baby had gone out the window. For the first year of double-duty Motherhood, I can honestly say that I doubted my abilities to connect to any kind of peace parenting style, (i.e. using a calm and gentle voice and understanding at all times the boys' sometimes difficult emotions). Instead, I often found myself to be impatient and emotionally sensitive and, frankly, sometimes I felt sorry for myself. This was not what I imagined motherhood to be. Where was the time for yoga? Where was the time for me?

Then, after one particularly challenging day, I distinctly remember telling myself, "You've got to find your peace again; for you, for the boys, for our family." And then I remembered the simple advice a good friend had given me a few weeks before: She told me to look at my life and realize that I had made the choices that resulted in me being right where I was, at that very moment. Moreover, she said if I wanted to alter the moment, then I needed to visualize a new perspective and find "the good" again. I decided to combine my existing path as a yogi with the path of motherhood. The following are some of the mind shifts that I made over the course of a few months to help rekindle my relationship with my inner peace:

BREATHE INTO YOUR LIMITATIONS

For many, this is a hard one to face. After giving birth, our lives are not the same; our bodies are not the same. Period. Months after my first and second sons were born, it was really tough to do some of my favorite yoga asanas as I had done in the past. In yoga philosophy, one of the moral principles (*Yamas)* to follow during the practice is non-violence (*ahimsa*). I often tell my yoga students that the asanas are here to serve you; here to provide feedback to the parts of your body that need some extra love and attention. That being said, trying too hard to get our "old bodies" back or trying to force ourselves into postures we once performed with ease is, simply put, violence to the body.

There is a middle way, and that is to respect your body's limits while in a stretch and breathe into it. The intensity you feel while in a posture will let you know when you've reached your limit; on a scale of 1-10 (1 being the lowest intensity and 10 the highest), if you are at a 10, ease up to a 3 or 4 and breathe again. Breathing consciously with slow, deep inhalations and long, extended exhalations sends the message to our nervous system not to be alarmed and to stay calm while we make some gentle adjustments to the body.

EASE UP ON YOUR EXPECTATIONS: LET THE KIDS CRAWL ON YOUR BACK!

Having experienced those wonderful yoga courses, I longed for a quiet place to do yoga without distractions. If you have a special room like this in your home, especially if your kids are a bit older and will give you some quiet time, you are really blessed. But in my case, we live in a small city apartment in Seoul with no place to hide from each other. So when I first made the resolve to resume my practice, my kids wanted to crawl on my back every time I was in a downward dog. Initially, I found this frustrating. But then I thought, "They can't help it, they're kids! Let them join!" Now that they are a bit older, they are occasionally too busy to notice when Mom is enjoying some "me time" on the mat. On most days, however, they can't resist joining me, and when the spirit moves us, we add sounds. Here's a few of our favorite.

- Cobra (*hissssssss* — usually followed by us slithering around the floor.)

- Tree Posture, or as Sebastian calls it, "The Flamingo" (*wind blowing and swaying tree sound*)

- Downward Dog (*barking sounds*)

- Happy Baby (*funny baby sounds — any emotion that arises*)

Be open to making up some new names for yoga postures with your kids, too.

A LITTLE BIT OF YOGA CAN MAKE ALL THE DIFFERENCE

Being a new Mother can be really hard on the muscles and joints. This is especially true if you are practicing attachment parenting and/or keeping the babes close to your chest for on-demand breast feeding (this can take a particularly heavy toll on your back!). For me, getting into a shoulder stand, a wide-legged forward bend, and a bow pose for even a few minutes helps alleviate much of the tightness that builds up in my trouble areas. But everyone experiences tightness in different spots, so you will have to explore a few postures that hit the sweet spot for you.

What if you are new to yoga and don't know where to begin? There are a lot of resources in your local library and on the Internet, (one of which I will mention below), to become familiar. However, if you want to get started now, here's a practice that I often find myself doing to help me reset and relax.

Warm up

- Start on your back and do a long body stretch with your arms stretched pass your head. Really stretching from your fingers down to your toes.

- Allow yourself a big inhalation and a long extended exhalation here. Begin to tune into your breathing and turn your attention inward.

- Pull your knees into your chest and extend arms out to the side and gently sway your hips from side to side to open up your lower back.

Mini Vinyasa Flow

- Table: Cat/Cow

- Downward Dog

- Plank Pose to Cobra

- Down Dog

(Do this sequence as many times as you like. If this is as far as you can get, which is sometimes the case for me, then keep the focus on your breathing and do every posture as consciously as you can)

27

Standing Postures (Asanas)

Warrior 1

Warrior 2 to Reverse Warrior

Triangle Pose

Wide-Legged Standing Forward Bend

Seated Spinal Twist

Shoulder Stand

Sivasana (Dead Man's Pose)

If you are unsure of how to position yourself in the postures above, and leaving the house is not an option, I recommend my favorite yoga website, called Yogaglo.com. It has over twenty-five quality teachers that post recorded yoga classes for a multitude of levels, styles, and time-durations. There is a small monthly fee, but if you consider the membership fees for gyms or yoga studios, it's totally worth it.

CLOSING BREATH

Spiritual growth often comes from challenging times, and parenting can be full of them. However, when we consciously nurture our bodies and give ourselves the inner attention we need and deserve, everyone benefits. The space you carve out in your life for yoga, or any form of physical development, nurtures your inner light. That same light shines on your children and enables them to grow in their own beautiful and unique ways. May you find peace and rekindle your light. ~Namaste.

Christine Cunningham

Christine Cunningham is an author and freelance outdoor writer dedicated to wildlife conservation and preservation, through providing opportunities to connect women to the outdoors. She shares the benefits of a fully-integrated outdoor lifestyle, through leading Alaska wilderness retreats and instructing hunter education courses in waterfowling and upland hunting for both women and youth. She serves on the board of WomenHunters and represents women in the outdoors as ProStaff for EvoOutdoors.

Her most recent book *Women Hunting Alaska* is available from Northern Publishing and on Amazon. She can be reached at cunningham@ yogaforduckhunters.com

✉ cunningham@yogaforduckhunters.com

🏠 www.yogaforduckhunters.com

🏠 www.womenhunters.com

🏠 www.evooutdoors.com

🏠 www.tonyruss.com/PageBook-WomenHuntingAlaska.html

LESSON 3

Nurtured by Nature—
Reclaiming Sacred Spaciousness

By Christine Cunningham

~~~

For years, my drive to work took me over a bridge that crossed a world-famous fishing river. Some mornings, I glanced over at the sunrise, latte in hand, to notice the mountains in the distance and the grassy tidal flats on either side of the road. There were many mornings I did not remember driving to work. My mind was filled with the noise of unproductive thinking. My relationship with the landscape I crossed over each morning was non-existent. It didn't matter that visitors travelled from all over the world to fish the river or that the flats were sacred ground to a small group of duck hunters. I had no idea what attracted them, what I might be missing, or even that it was calling to me.

At that time in my life, I lived by the clock. My dreams were interrupted by an alarm un-affectionately named "the Daily Grind," and which made the musical sound of wooden bars struck by mallets. Distractions continued throughout my day, amidst an endless, anxious struggle to complete tasks with energy and enthusiasm. There was a sense of emptiness in the captivity of every space I occupied—my office, my car, my home, and even within my own body. As much as my spiritual practice provided balance, and the calming voice of my yoga instructor echoed my deepest values—effort and achievement—it was another voice that invited me duck hunting. What followed changed my life.

Venturing out onto the flats for the first time, I discovered they were teeming with wild life. Buried in their grasses were blinds grown into the vegetation. Although they appeared from a distance to be an accidental accumulation of junk brought in with the tide, the blinds were fostered with the care of Japanese gardens. Dragonflies covered by the morning dew awaited the sun to dry their wings, caribou emerged from their beds to meet the morning, birds of prey lit on stumps to scan the flats for mice and the water for fish. A new world showed itself to me, one full of activity and timelessness. I wanted to learn what this world would teach me.

Developing a practice centered on nature offers a new paradigm, one that replaces that which is solely human and intentional with that which encompasses the entire living world. When we approach the outdoors with the same beginner's mind as our yoga practice, we quickly learn the benefit is not in the postures we attain but in the effort involved in attaining them. Whether our sacred places are in a church, synagogue, studio, office, or alongside a wild river stream, it is our sacred path and the innocent eye we bring to it that provides us with the value. The natural world offers the oldest remedy to the one we've built and an opening to expand the horizon of our awareness, explore wild spaces, and an awaking to the joy and beauty of being truly alive.

For the next ten years, my desire to learn from nature focused my vision, so instead of just watching nature, I was participating in it. I trained and followed bird dogs, spent nights camping out on the floor of remote duck shacks, and rafted down wild rivers a hundred miles from the nearest civilization. While writing about these adventures for outdoor publications, I met other women who chose to cultivate a similar life outdoors. Many of them were mothers who were passionate about incorporating their children into an outdoor lifestyle, sharing their delight in nature, and providing sustainable food options offered by gardening, fishing, and hunting.

DISCOVERING OUR SACRED SPACE IN NATURE

Each of us may recall a time in our childhood when we were outside — curious, stimulated, and safe. When we awake in the morning feeling unrested, and our first thoughts of the day are on what needs to be done, we can take this moment to refocus our energy on the symphony of nature stored deep within our being. We can hear the river rushing wild within us, the wind blowing across a field and through our hair, the smell of the fertile earth. When our spirit finds this sacred space, it reunites us with our true being and we are refreshed.

A good first step on any path is to do something that breaks our routine. Just stepping out into the air first thing in the morning, we can see the living world is everywhere we may not always look—it grows in the cracks of the sidewalks, it nests in trees and eaves, it stores food for winter, and it leaves its tracks in the snow. If we focus on just one square foot of soil, grass, bark, or water, we see a microcosm at work.

A simple retreat from the world in solitude and nature removes us from the daily environment that engenders routine and reactive thinking. A few breaths of outdoor air, the feel of the temperature on our skin, or meditation in nature provides a focus for our senses. This simple "reset" prepares us for our daily encounters. If we can find and foster this sacred spaciousness within ourselves, listen and feel the natural world around and within us, we are restored and ready for whatever adventure the day brings.

A SLOW WALK WITHOUT A DESTINATION

A friend once told me her husband appreciated her going on long walks because she "walked the meanness out." At the time, it just seemed like a funny thing to say, but there was truth to it. There is no place for anger in the outdoors. A slow walk in the woods or carefree wandering without a destination forces most feelings into exile. When the body is at work, it often does the work of our mind.

Any time spent in nature provides a new orientation to the world we live in and a new way of responding to daily events and challenges. A long walk in the silence of the outdoors is essentially a journey inward. It provides a physical benefit, but it also distills our emotional world, offering a counter pose to our sense of home. On these walks, we stretch our minds, bodies, and spirits and return to our homes, refreshed and with gratitude for the gift of life.

DRAWING CREATIVITY FROM NATURE

Nature restores us, but it also revitalizes us. Collecting leaves, rocks, pinecones, or antler sheds to incorporate into our homes or sanctuaries brings texture and meaning to our creative spaces. Building and tending a rock cairn by stacking stones symbolic of something in our lives helps us achieve a literal balance. When we surround ourselves with reminders of our natural environment, we honor a sanctuary of solitude in which we can retreat to slow down and come to quietude.

My first connection to nature as a source of truth was in writing nature-inspired haiku, a Japanese form of poetry with three lines. As I sat in the woods with pen and paper, my eyes landed on an old oak tree, and I was filled with inspiration. Whether taking our homework, yoga practice, painting hobby, or journaling outdoors, the abundance of nature enhances our creative processes.

NOTHING IN NATURE IS DIRTY—GET DIRTY!

When we choose the outdoors as our place of practice, we will no doubt trade some of the comforts of indoor spaces for the freedom and expansiveness of an outdoor environment. Some of the greatest blessings come to us when we overcome a natural resistance to cold, wet, or dirty environments. These are the joyful moments when we "break free" of our inhibitions and we are "wide open" to receive all life offers. This is when we sing and dance in the rain, throw our arms in the air after a sweaty victory to rejoice, or laugh with a friend after we have dared to roll down a hill on a school playground at the age of thirty-six.

Oftentimes, while watching people leave a building, I see their reaction to the weather outside. In cold and rainy weather, we often pull up our shoulders and our muscles become clenched and guarded. We unintentionally broadcast the message: "I just want to get through this awful part." When I find myself doing this, I remind myself to be open to what life offers. My muscles relax, my face lifts to invite the rain, and I stick out my tongue to taste the snow, or slow my pace to enjoy the smells of fall.

Letting go of the habit of reaction, distraction, or performance allows us to be truly alive and aware—a wild person in a wild place. When we cultivate the sacred spaciousness of nature within ourselves, start our day with nature, or come home from time spent outside, we are refreshed and ready to share our restored intuition, joy, and creativity with our families.

Harriet Winograd

BA, Art History, University of Wisconsin; AAS Apparel Design, Fashion Institute of Technology; MA, Art Education, New York University; MA, Art Therapy, Springfield College; MA, Integrative Health and Healing (currently pursuing), The Graduate Institute; Adjunct Faculty, Art History, University of Hartford.

Artist, Art Therapist, Art Educator, Dress Designer, winner of numerous art awards, including First Prize, Pen & Brush Club, NYC; First Prize, West Hartford Art League.

Most recently works in elder care as an art therapist.

✉ artsider@me.com

⨍ www.facebook.com/harriet.winograd

ⓟ www.pinterest.com/Vidabrevis

ⓘ www.linkedin.com/pub/harriet-winograd/8/b94/873

☏ 860 869 1921

Location: West Hartford, Connecticut, USA

The Art of Becoming a Grandmother

By Harriet Winograd

~~~

I am about to become a grandmother. I have two daughters, both of whom are having babies who will be three months apart in age. In preparation for these two births, I've been reading numerous books about grandparenthood. The overriding theme of these books is "don't give *any* unsolicited advice, and even when asked, be careful not to overstep." Despite these admonitions, I am incredibly excited and somewhat apprehensive. For instance, what am I to be called? I know of some women who do not want to be called "grandma." It makes them feel old, but I have no such problem. I am, after all, sixty-seven years old and have been waiting a long time for these blessed events.

Becoming a grandmother, however, has added another dimension to my concerns about aging, body image, and identity. For example, the other day I started wondering if I should stop coloring my hair because of my new status. I doubt that will happen, but the thought gave me pause. My life, since the age of fifty, has been marked by significant changes—menopause, divorce, aging and dying parents, and children leaving the nest. I have been an artist my whole life, and to cope with all these changes, I went back to school to get a master's degree in art therapy. My studies, papers, and research helped me to learn how to use my art to express the hurt, anger, and loss I was feeling.

While in that program, I took a class called "Therapeutic Aspects of Clay" and made a series of broken hearts. My favorite was a sculptural representation of the human heart, sliced and laid out on butcher paper for the world to see. It was *my* heart, and it was very disturbing to see it so chopped up; but it gave me great satisfaction to visually expose the pain that I could not express in words.

Much of my work is about the female figure in both 2D and 3D formats. In these works, I love to explore duality—both the beauty and the ugliness. One of my sculptural figures is a life-size torso covered in flesh tone lace that evokes an appreciation of the classic female nude in all its external perfection. As the viewer draws near, however, it becomes apparent that the torso is hollow. And, like an Iron Maiden, it has bloody spikes, protruding into the empty core. The contrast between the exterior and the interior illustrates the thread that has run so true through my art and life: I have had to learn that I cannot judge peoples' insides by what is happening on their outsides.

For example, in my own life, I felt I had the American dream: a successful husband, two beautiful children, two homes, and exciting vacations all over the world. But then the dream ended. Not only did the dream end, I discovered that my identity as a successful mother and wife was squelched, and I had to find a new way to be a parent and a person. Once again, I turned to art to express my feelings; one of my paintings from that time is of a pile of smoldering ashes where smoke from the burning remains of our former life are transformed into line drawings of my two daughters and myself. The name of the painting is "The Phoenix," and like the mythological bird, we survived and, dare I say, thrived.

In my former life, I was a stay-at-home mom who kept busy outside the home with part-time art teaching and volunteer activities. It was a wonderful time for me. My husband and I had a very traditional marriage. He made the money and I took care of the children and the home. I don't remember ever feeling overwhelmed by all the constant household routines. (I do remember once having to leave an unfinished painting to cook dinner and thinking that Picasso wouldn't have had to deal with such things.)

When the dream ended, I found myself divorced with one daughter away at college and the other in high school. My life had changed dramatically. Dinnertime was especially hard because that had always been the highlight of our day as a family. For me, it was not only the mealtime togetherness, but the loss of the comforting structure of menu planning, shopping, and cooking. When my younger daughter went away to boarding school, and I was left alone, every bit of that structure was gone.

During this time, I found I had to be healthy for myself, as well as for my girls. Raising female adolescents is not easy, even during the best situations. We had some difficult times as we moved from mistrust to trust, and anger to acceptance. Our therapist had to remind me many times that I was the grown up, even if I did not always feel that way.

We are now three grown women. My daughters are about to have their own daughters. Have I given them what they need to do what someone has called "good enough mothering"? Will their becoming mothers bring us closer? Somebody recently told me that being a grandparent is the only thing in life that is not overrated. Will that be my experience? What kind of grandmother will I be?

In the midst of all these changes, I began to experience aging in my body. Like it or not, I was becoming "the grandmother!" I had to stop wearing heels and needed to buy wide-toed "granny" shoes. My mouth started getting those mannequin lines and jowls on my jaw! My hair was thinning, and my middle was widening. I started having a hard time finding clothes. I've always worn junior sizes and they were looking too youthful and were not fitting the same way. "Women's" clothing looked too matronly. I was totally perplexed about what to wear. I have always been healthy, and I started having issues, such as cataract surgery, gall bladder removal, kidney stones, and new aches and pains. I suddenly realized I was confronting the conflict between our culture's fixation on youth and the reality of aging.

We all know that our culture tries to sell us the idea that aging is controllable, and that looking young for women is an important life mission. If cosmetic lotions can't do the job, then it's cosmetic surgery. I, however, have always loved the Japanese aesthetic of "wabi-sabi" that finds beauty in imperfection, accepting the cycle of growth, decay, and death as an integral part of life. Richard Powell, the author of *Wabi-Sabi Simple*, writes: "We are beautiful because we exist, and we learn to appreciate the beauty of our quirks and flaws—our scars, our stretch marks, and signs of aging—rather than buying into our culture's worship of 'flawless' youth."

I suppose that part of my perspective on aging is due to being born in the first year of the Baby Boomer generation. We post-WWII babies created quite a cultural revolution in our youth in the 1960s. We are now moving from midlife into elder-hood. This requires looking at our lives from a different perspective, and one of the marks of the Baby Boomers is a commitment to lifelong learning. I share that and am currently pursuing a master's degree in Integrative Health and Healing, where I am combining my work as an artist with my interests in healthy aging.

Making art has been my way of shaping my quest for self-identity and, yes, my self-identity is in flux once again, for I am about to become a grandmother. I am looking forward with great anticipation to sharing my artistic gifts with my new grandchildren. As this unfolds, what will my granddaughters unlock within me? What wellsprings of passion and compassion will I discover? Will I learn even more depths of love for my daughters as *they* enter the eternal cycle of birth and new life?

When my own grandmother died, my beloved Bubbe Gussie, and her family gathered at the Shiva, my cousins and I confessed to each other that we all thought we were her favorite even though she had never said that. In those special moments together, we learned a lesson. She taught us that the power of a grandmother's love was displayed not by word alone but by all the tangible gifts she gave us: her hugs and kisses, homemade blintzes, uproarious card games, and her adoring smile. From her we learned the true art of being a grandmother. I hope to be remembered that way, and *my* gifts will be different. They will be mine, born of my life and work as an artist, a mother, and a grandmother.

Christine Bové

Feng Shui expert Christine Bové inspires women to allow creative energies to flow into their environments and mindsets to improve their confidence, bring clarity to their future, and set them up for success. Christine has spent most of her life studying and enjoying fashion and design and ultimately found her passion with a career as a Feng Shui expert. To learn more about Christine, visit www.christinebove.com and sign up for her five Feng Shui Video Tips to enhance your Mind, Body, and Home and create the success you desire.

🏠 **www.christinebove.com**

LESSON 5

Feng Shui for Moms: How to manage the flow in your home

By Christine Bové

~~~

From chaos to clutter, how do you manage your home with so many personal energies living together? Some may be more sensitive to clutter while another may be your clutter bug. The key to balancing it all as a mom is understanding we all have a different style personality and honoring those personal energies.

What is Feng Shui and why does it matter? Feng Shui is the understanding that your environment affects and reflects what's going on in your life. When your environment is out of balance with clutter and chaos, it is a clear sign that other areas of your life are out of balance, too. Applying Feng Shui principles can help you keep your life in balance and improve the energy of your home.

Although, I'm not a mom yet, I have eight nieces and nephews and spent my teenage years babysitting. I have a lot of experience with children, from changing diapers to sleepovers. From my experience, I know managing your home and lifestyle with kids is not an easy task.

Organizing your home and children's rooms may be a challenge for the mom who is super organized but the rest of your family is not, or vice versa. Maybe one child is the clutter bug and the other isn't. So what do you do?

First, you need to honor everyone's energy and surrender to the idea you have to change them. The more you push to change someone, the more resistance you will meet.

WHO'S IN CHARGE?

In Feng Shui, it's easy to see who's in charge of a home by reviewing the space. If children's toys are dominating the home showing up in every room in the home, it's clear the children are running the house. In my consultations, I can quickly tell when a mom shares her struggles and frustrations, that the kids clearly dominate. The solution is to designate two spaces for the kid's toys—their rooms and a playroom or family room. For some, this is easy. For others it's a challenge, due to lack of space, but it is a good rule of thumb. The idea is not to judge but to correct what the underlying imbalance is. You can ask some questions: Are the toys being used every day? Do the children respect what they have? Do the children know how to pick up after themselves? The key is to acknowledge the underlying reason for the clutter so you can change it.

Now, this is not going to happen overnight. You need to approach this day by day. First, start by noticing what toys your children play with every day—this includes the teenager's stuff. Take notice of what they use every day and what they haven't touched in a while. Take those things and put them in a box and place them in a closet with an expiration date of thirty days. Notice do the children request these items? If not, it may be the time to donate them. Or you can create a system of rotation—switching them out on a regular basis. This is a great way to ensure all the toys in the home are valued and respected by the child. This can save you time and money. When your children ask for new things, you just take from your secret stash and boom, they have "new" toys!

Teach your children that for each item that comes home, something must be given away. I teach my clients to always buy things you love, need, and have a space for. If you apply these tips with your children, you will maintain the clutter. Again, it's something you practice over and over, and you may not always meet this tip with great success. But the more you practice this new concept and teach your children, the easier it will become. You need to be persistent in the beginning of creating a new habit, but if you do it for thirty days, just think of the reward it will bring to you!

DECORATING YOUR CHILDREN'S ROOM

For the little ones, the key is to see everything through their eyes. Get down on the floor to see from their eye level. Take in how the room feels from the decor, the shelves, what is placed where, etc. Make sure to do this at night. You want to see what they are seeing. To you, the room may feel fun and childlike but what does it feel like for the little girl/boy? You may discover what's keeping them up at night, like the streetlight that peers into the room and beams on the teddy bear's eyes that makes him look really scary. Decorate for a child from their eye level.

BED PLACEMENT AND WHY BUNK BEDS ARE A FENG SHUI "NO-NO"

In the early years, from ages one through three, it's best to keep the beds up against the wall to give children a nurturing supportive feeling. After about three years old, it's good to shift the bed so there is space on both sides, with a solid wall behind their head. This places them in the command position, which relaxes their nervous system, as they can see everything happening in the room. A good solid headboard is best, with two end tables on either side for balance. It's best to clear all clutter from under the bed, as items under the bed can impact the child's ability to sleep through the night. If you must use under-the-bed drawers, use them for clothing and bedding. In a perfect world, there would be no electronics in the bedroom, but that's becoming a bigger challenge these days. If you have an overly sensitive child and he/she is having issues sleeping at night, it's best to keep all electronics as far as possible from their bed. Take note of what is on the other side of the wall where they sleep, such as electrical outlets, electronics, etc. All this can have an impact on their sleep and moods.

One tip that I have found very successful is no bunk beds, even those with desks instead of beds underneath. I've seen 98 percent success rate every time I recommend taking apart the bunk beds. One of my very first clients had four girls in one room, so you can imagine how much fun that could be. Her second daughter was sharing bunk beds with her older sister, and it clearly was a problem. The mother shared how unhappy her daughter was. I brought to her attention the impact of bunk beds and the negative energy her youngest daughter was probably feeling from sleeping underneath her older sister. The mom agreed and we decided on a new arrangement for the room without bunk beds. The very next day, I received one of most unforgettable calls! It was my client raving with joy that she had a new daughter! From a moody teenager to a happy one, her daughter was a like a new person.

Another client had a bunk bed with the desk situated under the bunk bed for their computers. Her son only slept on the top bunk the first night and never again. I explained about the energy of the electronics in the room and under his bed. He just couldn't handle this energy underneath him every night.

WHAT TO DO WITH THEIR ARTWORK?

The second challenge I hear from moms is—what am I supposed to do with all their artwork? You have to learn how to determine what to keep and what to discard. Sure, you can pack up everything they ever make in boxes and store them in your attic (however, please note your attic represents your future), but what's the point of putting it all in boxes if no one is going to look at or it just gets thrown out when your child grows up and moves out? A good plan is to go through their items together at the end of each school day, or every week. Let the child pick out the items they love. Then designate one area in your home—the playroom, kitchen, or their room—to display their artwork. If you really love it, frame it or put it in a portfolio book to keep on the shelf to share with friends and family when they visit. Consider giving some of the pieces to friends or family as little gifts from the children. Simply displaying their stuff can have such a positive impact on a child's self-esteem. It shows how much you value their creative side.

Stop aiming for perfection and accept that your space won't always be spotless and organized when you have a family living in the home. The key is to be sure that everyone is clear on their space and make sure it is always respected.

Teresa Baker

Teresa Baker is the owner of Wellness Essentials in Fort Madison, Iowa. She offers individuals integrative wellness for the whole person, an opportunity for personal and spiritual growth, cultivating awareness, and transforming consciousness. She worked in the medical field as a RN for over twenty years, is a licensed massage therapist, holistic health coach, and holds certifications in Colon Therapy, Energy Healing, and Advanced Theta Healing. Teresa is very passionate about the evolution and development of the whole self, enjoys teaching, and sharing knowledge with others while empowering them to pursue their own journey to divine health.

✉ dtbaker@geticonnect.com

🏠 www.yourwellnessessentials.com

f www.facebook.com/yourwellnessessentials.com

LESSON 6

Living From the Rhythm of Your Heart

By Teresa Baker

~~~

Walk with me won't you, to a beautiful spot in nature that you love. Sit quietly and be still. Close your eyes. Then, take a few deep breaths, place your hand on your heart, and feel the rhythm of your heart beating. Can you feel it? Now, silently give gratitude for everything in your life thus far that has showed up, no matter what you perceive as good or bad. Then ask the divine creator, "What is my divine mission here on Earth, and what do I need to know? Show me." Your answer will come, and it may be in ways you never dreamed of. Do you ever feel like there is something magnificent inside you waiting to be birthed, but it feels like outside influences and factors seem to keep it hidden and prevent it from emerging? Well, the good news is there is something wonderfully divine deep inside you. It has always been there waiting for you to remember. The heart contains your unique instructions in life. When you live from your intuition, your decisions and perceptions change.

Today, I would like you to consider and embrace the idea that you can create an amazing life—a life you have always imagined, by releasing old patterns of thoughts and beliefs that keep you stuck from reaching your highest potential. You are a precious being and you were born with magical and unique gifts, talents, blessings, and challenges that no other person on the planet encompasses. Yes, there are people who may have similar gifts but none identical to yours. Within you exists an original blue print waiting to be awakened.

BE OPEN TO EXPLORATION

Being a mom is one of the most difficult yet rewarding professions in the world. How many times have we all heard that? Well, I believe it is true. Yet, we mothers tend to get lost in the mix, working so feverishly, doing for everyone else, and forgetting our core truth of who we really are and what special uniqueness we bring to the world. Many of us moms don't even hold the belief that we are special and unique, or we may hold many distorted beliefs that were handed down to us from parents and ancestors. And we react and interact in ways that reflect those beliefs, not even questioning them or asking ourselves if they are even true. Often times, these beliefs are based on fear, not love, thereby distorting our view of ourselves, and distorting our interactions with others, and we end up only living a small fraction of our true potential.

So where does a busy mom start who has so many irons in the fire? Reread the first couple sentences of this chapter. When you ask, you will receive the answer. The answer may show up as a sudden awareness about a characteristic, belief, or trait you have that you don't necessarily embrace. Having that awareness is a first step and key, for it may propel you into searching and seeking for ways to change or enhance your wellbeing. Staying open to exploring, learning, and receiving divine guidance helps point the way, and it cannot be over emphasized. Perhaps it will lead you to a book, author, a documentary, a mentor, teacher, healer, or healing modality that you had never heard of, or considered to seek out. If it shows up, it may just be your answer.

Being a young mother of three amazing sons (who are now grown) was an enormous challenge and a huge blessing for me. They taught me so much about love, compassion, responsibility, forgiveness, humor, hard work, organization, fun, focus, dedication, devotion, imagination, and so much more. With all these amazing things I was learning and feeling about being a mom, I also had those dreaded negative thoughts and distorted beliefs about myself and the world that held me back. Although, I did not know at the time they were distorted, or were not for my highest good. I simply didn't know. A few things that I did know: I had a very curious mind; I loved learning, listening, and exploring anything around self-awareness, self-improvement, and self-empowerment. I also had a huge love for all things regarding health, wellness, and nutrition. I may not have always reflected those things 100 percent of the time in my life, but I was very passionate about them and I still am to this day.

It was not until years later (after my children were getting much older and my mind became more still without all the distractions that go into motherhood and being a wife) that many doors started opening for me, and I started to receive answers to many questions I had pondered a good portion of my life. I believe by remaining open-minded, curious, and receptive, the answers began to show up. I always loved to read. But time was always an issue, and I began to read as if I was making up for lost time. I have a love affair with books, and my book collection of wellness, prevention, nutrition, health, mystical, esoteric, and spiritual studies has grown considerably over the years. I immersed myself in research, self-study, and began to attend classes, seminars, and workshops—many focused on self-improvement, consciousness, health, healing, and energy. These were all wonderful gifts and changes I made, which had a profound effect on my life and the way I view and embrace it.

That old saying, "just make one small change," sounds so cliché. But I realized how true it really was. I made profound changes in my diet even though I thought I was always pretty healthy. I stepped up my game. I began incorporating a lot of greens and juicing into my daily routine. I began incorporating detoxifying strategies, getting rid of toxic chemicals in and around the house, switched to more "ecofriendly" products, began meditating (going on almost 4 years now), spent more time appreciating and being in nature, and became very intentional about what I would and wouldn't allow into my life—everything from music to food to people. Every change I made or would discover would lead to another discovery or door to open. It was truly magical! Abundance of blessings and synchronicities started to show up everywhere.

Though all of these changes were paramount to where I am today, nothing compares to the healing that took place when I found out how our limiting beliefs and subconscious programs can hold us back. It was icing on the cake to what I had already been experiencing. We can do all the juicing in the world and eat the right diet, and those are all great things, but when our beliefs about ourselves and the world are distorted and not supporting our highest good, we truly do not live out our original divine blue print. Every symptom in the body and every stressful experience in life represent emotional patterns of reaction stemming from the subconscious mind. Most of us don't even realize the subconscious mind is even there, or its purpose. The subconscious mind has a Soul purpose of protection and speaks with symptoms as a means to inform you that you now have the ability to think, feel, and act with love.

Your brain was wired by your parents and society by the time you were seven years old. Mostly with limited beliefs that only reflected your parents or societies frame of reference or perceptions. Beliefs function like computer programs, creating health or sickness, happiness or depression, wealth or poverty, success or failure, loneliness or connectedness, and thereby create our daily experiences of the world around us. Most of the beliefs we hold onto are beneath our conscious awareness. Some are formed during our childhood experiences. Others are passed down through generations in our DNA, and some through the collective unconscious. So much what we think our beliefs are, often times, are others' beliefs that get downloaded to us, and we react to situations that do not always serve us. We can pick these beliefs up from the media, television, newspaper, magazines, schools, churches, etc.

It was no accident that an amazing person showed up in my life that would share with me about limiting stuck beliefs and patterns. For this was how my life was flowing, and they would point the way for me to have many healing sessions — sessions to catapult my inner life for a more expanded, joyful, blissful existence. The healing continues to this day, and I was guided to become a Theta Healer. Theta Healing is a healing modality developed by Vianna Stibal that allows the practitioner to facilitate instant changes in a client's belief systems. It is a method used to release and reprogram limiting beliefs, habits, or issues, as well as assist with physical and emotional issues. Be prepared to be amazed! May you find your path, be filled with faith, and know how amazing and divinely perfect you are. Live in the Rhythm of your heart.

Lisa Shozuya

With a smart, creative and heart-strong approach, Lisa Shozuya embraces the mission-driven leader and reconnects them with their innate voice. By creating a concrete connection to their words, communication, and the POWER of their life story, she helps define big pictures so leaders may live, love, and lead the way they were meant to. To inquire about one-to-one coaching, schedule appearances, or to propose a collaboration event or retreat, email lisa@lisashozuya.com or connect at www.lisashozuya.com. She currently lives on the island of Oahu with her son Nicholas and serves clients in Hawai`i, the mainland USA, the UK, and other countries.

✉ lisa@lisashozuya.com

🏠 www.lisashozuya.com

LESSON 7

Three Keys to Living Your A-N-D

By Lisa Shozuya

~~~

When the pages of my life turned, I never imagined there would be a chapter on losing my voice. If you know anything about buried hopes and dreams, unfulfilled expectations, the "it's too late" syndrome, the "I'm too tired" syndrome, or even the "*I-have-secret-wishes-lost-in-the-black-hole-of-house-clutter-never-to-be-found-again*" avoidance, then I'm sure you will relate. This lesson is simple, powerful, and a gift that pays forward the bright and beautiful brilliance you deserve for the rest of your busy life.

Pre-mom days, my life was going to be the one with the fairytale ending. You know that storybook, right? The truth is the story I lived didn't come close to that expectation. As funny (or shocking) as this sounds, I actually got a download from the man upstairs that my fairytale *ending* was actually limiting me. Whaaaaat? Yep. There were pages—more like chapters—in my storybook that were being overlooked, turned without ever being read, lived without truly being expressed. The pages *in between* where three simple letters—A-N-D— seemed as invisible as I, myself, had become. I didn't see it at the time (and I don't think anyone else around me did either), but fortunately the signs were pronounced enough to truly awaken me. Little did I know that this interruption would change the course of my life as a mom and a woman, forever.

I remember the night so clearly. It was a breaking point. Or maybe more honestly, a breakthrough to the other side of something that I was finally ready to admit, finally ready to change, and finally ready to receive. I was in my room and tears were flowing. As a mom, you understand these days. It creeps up on us after trying so hard to do it all and be it all, so our family, our work, and everything else we are giving our time to can have it all. This cry felt different, though. I got weak in the knees and literally fell to the foot of my bed. The contents of my heart began pouring out onto the floor and wouldn't stop. I was always "the strong one," so this feeling of helplessness was not comfortable. I looked up with my eyes closed and my mind uttered, "God, if you exist..." words spoke out, "...just take me, I'm yours. I don't know what the heck I'm doing." I cried the hardest cry of my life then fell asleep. The next morning I felt lighter than I had in years. My son, who was four at the time, woke up just as he did every day—full of joy and exuberance for being alive, smiling with all his heart and soul, and giving me a hug that felt like he knew I needed it.

From that moment forward, I began unraveling those very things in me that were most tangled up. By continually bulldozing forward in life, I was building over entanglements that should have first been DE-tangled. I went back to the aspirations I put aside and immersed myself in water, so to speak, so I could gently swish and sway the tangles out. I was never one to see my glass half-empty but I somehow fooled myself into believing that an empty glass was a good thing. After all, I was doing it for my son, my family, my work. But I wasn't happy, healthy, or whole on the inside, and my outside was crumbling. I did the unthinkable. I let go of my fairytale ending and pointed my energy into healing—becoming the CEO of my own life and finding my *AND*—those unseen, unheard, and unknown pages of my story. What came of that made me a better mom than ever and began defining my work to the world. I mastered standing on the spot that God designed for me, and I did whatever it took to hold still and open myself to receiving. This created opportunities to live, love, and lead just as I was meant to—something only possible when living *into* the *AND* of your gorgeous life.

THREE KEYS TO LIVING YOUR *A-N-D*

First, remember the *AND* IS your life. The pages that you overlook, the hopes and dreams that you put aside, the things within that scream for your attention that can no longer be ignored. This is NOT about either or. This is about paying attention to what those important pages *in between* your family life and career are saying, because this is the exact point where we lose who we are—where our voices become silent as Moms.

KEY 1: "A" ~ AWAKEN + ARTICULATE

Speak. Take a deep breath and share your words out loud. It doesn't matter what they are. It is only important that you release them from inside you. This step takes practice and is all about feeling the burn like a workout, NOT burning out. Burn out happens when you tune out—*always*—so really tune in and listen to your own thoughts as you speak them. Instead of forcing positive thinking in order to combat negative thoughts, or ignoring your own needs to make up for the guilt of not giving enough at work or at home, do this:

- GO IN to the entanglements and like a reporter,
- AWAKEN the un-turned pages and
- ARTICULATE what you find.

Let your subconscious mind hear your needs, see your dilemma, and know how to support you. You do not have to understand how things will work out. You do not have to make anything happen. All you have to do is speak freely and get everything up and out so that anything out of order has the freedom and room to rearrange itself naturally and organically.

KEY 2: "N" ~ NOURISH + NOTE

Write. The "N" is where I teach clients to *let it rip*. This will help you to hear and heal the contents of your heart and soul. The act of NOTING will lead to NOURISHMENT. It just happens. For three days in a row, to start, write everything and anything that enters your mind on paper. It's not easy, but who said de-tangling a wad of anything was instantaneous? The pen to paper *action* is going to reach down into the metaphoric messy closet, the junk drawer you never look in, the pages you never thought to read, and pull out the fear of what it would be like to live your life…bright and beautiful. Trust your needs. They are designed to tell you exactly what nourishment your mind, body, and heart require. There is no need to look back at these pages. Just note it down, let the act of writing nourish you, and keep moving.

KEY 3: "D" ~ DEEPEN + DEFINE

Live. Once you get into the groove, something meaningful and fulfilling starts to occur. This is the point of full bloom. I LOVE the insides of flowers, just as I LOVE the insides of people. It's a power center. It is where the story of your life comes from and that's where all your answers are. We are all *constants* in our life…ever changing, ever growing, and ever finding our way back to who we are. It is a very DEEP way to live, and in my opinion, the most fulfilling. At every stage, you will find a groove, confidence, and ease about significant points in life that come, then go. When you started your career, how did it feel? When your child was born, what went through your mind? We tend to focus so much on the Point As and Point Bs in life, but what about the *AND* in between? Take the time to DEFINE those *AND*s then put all your discoveries into your words and your work. Your voice will emerge from a depth in you that you never knew you had. Guaranteed.

As you can see, these steps are not linear. Not one color, one note, or one-size-fits-all. They are fluid for a reason, continuous for a purpose, and meant to help you find your voice, articulate it, note it, and over time, truly define it. I promise if you start now, it will NOT take a whole lifetime to heal or as many years as you've been alive to catch up. It will happen quickly and, ironically, give you the structure needed to stop flying by the seat of your pants and start living from the seat of your soul.

I will leave you with one final hug to carry with you in your heart as you journey. There was a saying I unfolded for years through my healing: "No matter how far you are on the wrong path, GO BACK." I lived that every single day until my *AND*, the pages *in between*, emerged and became worth speaking, worth writing, worth living, and worth sharing. Now it's your turn. The world is waiting.

Anne Lowenthal

Anne Lowenthal, MPH, Holistic Health Coach, and Natural Health Educator, loves sharing her passion for and knowledge of essential oils and vegan macrobiotic cooking, and empowering women to reinvent their health care with safer, cheaper and more effective solutions for themselves and their families. Anne leads a team of Natural Health Educators and teaches classes, including Medicine Cabinet Makeover and Whole Foods Cooking with Essential Oils.

A graduate of the Institute of Integrative Nutrition, Anne is also a yoga instructor and sound healer and is certified in the AromaTouch Technique. She lives in Newton, MA, with her family.

✉ eomaven@gmail.com

⌂ www.annelowenthal.com

⌂ www.proessentialoils.com/beyourbestwellness

f www.facebook.com/anne.lowenthal.9

🐦 www.twitter.com/annelowenthal1

📌 www.pinterest.com/annelowenthal

in www.linkedin.com/in/annelowenthal

LESSON 8

Essential Oils: Nature's Medicine for Balance & Tranquility

By Anne Lowenthal

~~~

Gorgeous tropical setting, soothing spa treatments, and delicious food prepared for you. Is it easy to be relaxed in a setting like this? Yes, of course. Stuck home with sick, cranky, hungry kids, husband out of town, work deadlines looming, not so easy, right?

Even for those of us lucky enough to enjoy spa vacations occasionally, how do we bring peace and serenity to our daily chaotic lives? I doubt there is a mom out there who hasn't encountered stressful scenarios like these:

• Sleeping soundly, you're jolted awake by the shrieks of your baby who is burning up and grabbing at his ear.

• Driving late afternoon carpool to an after school activity, you're feeling so tired that you can barely keep your eyes open.

• It's bedtime, you're exhausted, yet your mind is racing and you just can't fall asleep.

As far back as I can remember, I've been interested in alternative/ holistic approaches to healthcare. I've explored many modalities to relieve stress and physical pain over the years from Ayurveda, acupuncture, chiropractic therapy, homeopathy, macrobiotics, and yoga. I've dragged my husband and my son to more alternative practitioners than I can count. I even formalized my exploration by completing not one, but two health coaching programs over the last several years. Yet my search continued for safe and effective solutions to rather minor wellness challenges, until I found Certified Pure Therapeutic Grade essential oils.

As a health coach and natural health educator, I meet moms all the time now who are looking for a different path to wellness for themselves and their families. They want safe and effective solutions to their most common health concerns. They are tired of side effects. They want to remove harmful chemicals from their homes. And they need simple self-care routines to stay healthy and happy.

WHAT ARE ESSENTIAL OILS?

They are aromatic compounds, steam distilled (or cold pressed from the rind, in the case of citrus oils) from plant material: flowers, bark, roots, leaves, etc. A particular essential oil is made up of hundreds of chemical compounds. The amount of a particular compound in an essential oil can vary a great deal depending on which species of the plant is used, where the plant is grown and harvested, and the particular weather and soil conditions. Quality matters since we breathe them, put them on our skin, and in some cases, take them internally.

Essential oils are produced and sold by many different companies. I use doTERRA essential oils. doTERRA is now the largest essential oil company in the world, and their testing exceeds industry standards. I trust you to do your own research and decide what's best for you. Many of my recommendations, such as using some essential oils internally, are based on using doTERRA, since most other brands of essential oils are not approved to be taken internally. The main ways you'll use them is aromatically, topically, internally, and for home cleaning and personal care products.

HOW MUCH DO I USE?

Frequency trumps amount. Essential oils are extremely concentrated. One drop of peppermint essential oil is equivalent to twenty-eight cups of peppermint tea! So we're generally using one or two drops at a time. But unlike with pharmaceuticals, you can use them more often. For acute issues, you can use every fifteen minutes as needed.

CAN ESSENTIAL OILS HELP ME SAVE MONEY?

Most essential oils cost only pennies per drop and are multi-purposeful. For instance, a bottle of peppermint essential oil can be used to soothe your toddler's stomach, bring down your baby's fever, relieve your headache, wake you up when you're falling asleep at your desk, freshen your breath, and cool you on a hot day, or when you're having hot flashes. If kept out of the heat and sunlight, it will last indefinitely.

HOW TO USE AROMATICALLY

Simply smell the oil from the bottle to get an aromatic benefit, but I can't emphasize enough the benefit of a diffuser. I have them all around my house! Diffusing essential oils eliminates airborne pathogens and has a rapid effect on our mood.

HOW TO USE TOPICALLY

The bottom of our feet is the best place to massage essential oils to get them into the system, unless you're looking for a localized effect. Then you would apply in a particular area. Always dilute with carrier oil, such as fractionated coconut oil, when using on young kids or on sensitive skin, or when using "hot" oils, like oregano or cassia. It's generally better to layer one essential oil over another rather than mix them, unless you understand the science of blending.

HOW TO USE INTERNALLY

The general guideline here is to limit internal use to essential oils with the Certified Pure Therapeutic Grade designation, and even then, only with oils that have a supplement facts label. A great way to get started using them internally is to add a drop of a citrus oil to your glass of water. (Please don't add them to plastic; use only glass or stainless.) Some oils, like oregano, are best taken therapeutically in a vegetable capsule. Many essential oils can be used for cooking; usually one drop is sufficient and sometimes, even less. Dip a toothpick into the bottle and swirl it into the food after cooking to get the desired flavor.

MORNING SELF-CARE

Do you wake up early and easily? Or is it a struggle each and every morning to get out of bed? Essential oils provide a non-caffeinated way to start the day. Massage a drop of peppermint oil into each foot first thing in the morning.

BEDTIME SELF-CARE

If you have young kids, you may not get any time alone the whole day. And by the time you've finished cleaning up after dinner, done the laundry, and packed lunches for the next day…you can't wait to crawl into bed. But then your mind starts racing, and you can't fall asleep. Sound familiar?

Applying essential oils topically at bedtime takes only seconds; yet they transform my bedtime routine into a mini spa treatment. I love to massage the oils into my feet before bed. It's the ultimate form of self-care. They smell wonderful and calming. While not greasy, they do soften the feet and they work quickly to quiet my mind. My favorites at bedtime are frankincense, lavender, vetiver, and doTERRA's Serene Calming Blend.

Running a diffuser with a timer (e.g., on for fifteen seconds every few minutes throughout the night) really helps with sleep as well. If you have the luxury and time to take a bath before bed, try adding a few drops of essential oil to your bath water.

DIY PROJECTS/RECIPES

A great place to start is www.doterrablog.com for lots of Do-It-Yourself (DIY) and recipe ideas. You will find colognes, personal care products, cleaning supplies, and gift and recipe ideas.

Here are two easy examples:

Natural Body Wash

Ingredients:

- 8 ounce pump bottle

- 1/2 cup unscented Castile soap

- 4 tablespoons vegetable glycerin

- 3 tablespoons fractionated coconut oil

- 10 drops of your favorite essential oil

Combine ingredients into glass pump bottle. Add desired essential oil(s). Shake to combine. You're done! Make sure to shake before each use, as the ingredients will separate.

Tip: For an uplifting body wash, try these essential oils: Peppermint, Grapefruit, Lime, or Eucalyptus. For a relaxing body wash, try these: Lavender, Bergamot, Geranium, or Roman Chamomile.

Peppermint Hot Chocolate

Add 1 drop of peppermint essential oil to 1 cup of hot chocolate and stir.

PRECAUTIONS:

- Essential oils should never be used directly in the eyes or ears.

- Certain essential oils, like oregano (a potent natural antibiotic) are "hot" and can burn the skin. Dilution with carrier oil, such as fractionated coconut oil, is a must. And for internal use, hot oils should be taken in a vegetable capsule.

- Citrus oils make our skin photosensitive, and therefore, we shouldn't use them on areas of the skin that will be exposed to the sun over the next one to three days.

- NEVER use water to dilute an essential oil; ALWAYS dilute with a vegetable oil, such as fractionated coconut oil, if you experience any discomfort or are using on a young child or sensitive skin.

- The information here is for educational purposes only and is not meant to diagnose, treat, prevent, or cure any disease. Use essential oils with knowledge and caution. If you are receiving treatment for any condition, check with your health care professional before attempting to self-treat with essential oils.

Hopefully this lesson will be just the beginning of your foray into essential oils. Resources abound, and I would love to help educate and empower you to use essential oils for self-care and to improve your daily life. Please check out my Facebook page for tips on using essential oils, and contact me with your questions. Most of all, have fun as you explore the world of nature's medicine!

Ellen Allard

Ellen has a BA in Music Education, Boston University, an MA in Education, Arcadia University, and a Certification in Health Coaching from IIN. She owns Gluten Free Diva Health Coaching and 80-Z Music, Inc. She helps people get healthy, gluten free and otherwise, and she is a touring musician, performing family concerts and presenting workshops for teachers on the importance of music for young children. For a free pdf featuring three of Ellen's most requested gluten free recipes, sign up for her newsletter at www.glutenfreediva.com.

🏠 www.glutenfreediva.com

🏠 www.ellenallard.com

f www.facebook.com/glutenfreediva

🐦 www.twitter.com/gfhealthcoach

📌 www.pinterest.com/gfdiva

in www.linkedin.com/in/ellenallard

A Happy Gluten Free Belly

By Ellen Allard

~~~

Imagine being a kid with a happy belly. You go to birthday parties and you get to eat pizza and cupcakes like all the other kids. When you go to family celebrations, there's always food for you to eat. Your parents pack your lunch for school in really cool lunch bags, and whenever you go on a play date, your friends always have food for you to eat at their houses. And even though there are lots of things you can't eat, everyone in your family and school helps you to feel like you're just one of the gang.

If you're a kid with Celiac Disease or a Gluten Intolerance, and you're lucky enough to have a life where gluten free is par for the course and your family and friends and teachers and other grownup people in your life are on your team, you just might be that kid with a happy belly.

GLUTEN FREE IS EVERYWHERE

By now, you probably know someone who is gluten free. You've seen gluten free menus popping up at all of your favorite restaurants, and your grocery store has a gluten free section. Did you know that it's one of the fastest growing segments in the food industry? That's because there are a lot of people jumping on the gluten free bandwagon and thus, there's a lot of money to be made. But while there are some who want to try going gluten free just to see what it's all about, there are others who must adhere to a strict gluten free diet because of a Celiac Diagnosis or they've been tested positive for or have anecdotal evidence that they are gluten intolerant. For these people, this is serious business.

A PLACE TO START

While you may have suspected an issue with gluten as a result of stomach aches after your child eats bread, pizza, and pasta, there are other telltale signs, including but not limited to bloating, diarrhea, constipation, fatigue, constant ear infections and colds, headaches, and mood swings. You might want to start by asking your medical professional to have your child tested for Celiac. You can also try an elimination diet, but the risk in doing this is that once your child has been gluten free and finds relief, the only way to confirm Celiac is to have him or her go back to eating gluten.

KNOWLEDGE IS POWER

Gluten is a protein found in wheat, rye, barley, and any products made with these grains. But it's not just the obvious like bread and pasta and cookies and muffins and cake and pancakes. It can hide in things like vitamins, medications, bouillon, toothpaste, glue on envelopes, licorice, lipstick, beer, French fries, salad dressings, seasoned rice mixes, imitation crabmeat (like you might find in a California Roll from your favorite Japanese restaurant), and cereal. Oats can be contaminated, depending on where they're grown or stored. Play dough can contain gluten if made with wheat.

And then there's cross contamination. An otherwise safe gluten free food becomes unsafe when it comes into contact with gluten. For example, French fries are gluten free unless they've been sprinkled with flour to keep from sticking during manufacturing, or fried in oil used to fry food breaded with wheat.

While there is a dizzying list of foods, cosmetics, personal hygiene products, and more that contain gluten, armed with information, the gluten free life becomes manageable. Knowledge is your best ally. Become your child's advocate. Learn what to look for when reading labels. Consider hiring a health coach who specializes in helping people go gluten free. You can join a local Celiac support group, participate in online Celiac forums, and visit websites, like www. celiac.com and www.celiaccentral.org, to learn all of the ins and outs of going gluten free. Visit online blogs (www.glutenfreediva.com, www.elanaspantry.com, www.adventuresofaglutenfreemom.com, www.glutenfreemom.com) for recipes and stories of how others manage being gluten free.

A GLUTEN FREE FAMILY AFFAIR

While it is a very personal decision, I believe that the most loving gesture for your gluten free child is for everyone in your family to go gluten free while at home. Is this challenging? Can it help your child adjust to the hardship of going gluten free? Will there be stumbling blocks? Are there ways to get support as this transition is being made? Yes, absolutely. You can't put a price tag on the love that your child will feel in knowing that members of his or her family have made the decision to be gluten free.

You can also start a blog on which you and your child can post recipes and pictures of food you make together, or new gluten free foods you find at the grocery store. Buy a nice assortment of to-go containers and insulated bags so that gluten free food can easily be transported when meals are eaten outside of your home.

A HAPPY GLUTEN FREE BELLY

Raising my own two adult daughters and watching them raise their kids has taught me how important it is to learn about basic nutrition (including, but not limited to, gluten free) and also to listen to their complaints when they don't feel well. We all want our children to have happy bellies.

One of the quickest ways to a happy gluten free belly is to serve healthy, kid-friendly gluten free food that you know will have your child doing cartwheels and high fives. Some suggestions include Annie's Gluten Free Rice Pasta & Cheddar Mac & Cheese, Food Should Taste Good Crackers, Mary's Gone Crackers, and pizza made with Udi's Pizza Crust. There are hundreds of blogs online that feature gluten free recipes. Get creative and figure out how to make your favorite family recipe gluten free. Try this simple gluten free snack:

MINI BANANA NUT CHOCOLATE PIZZA

Make sure the nut butter and chocolate is gluten free.

One banana, cut into 1" slices

Nut butter of choice (peanut, almond, sunflower, walnut etc.)

Chocolate chips or chocolate bar

Spread one side of banana slices with nut butter. Place on cookie sheet with nut butter side facing up. Drizzle melted chocolate on nut butter side of banana. Freeze until chocolate has just solidified and serve one soon-to-be happy gluten free belly.

JOURNEY TO HEALTH

As a child, I was always hungry. My parents thought I was always in the middle of a growth spurt. This hunger, however, continued into adulthood, even after meals that would've satisfied any normal appetite. In my late 40s, when I shared this with my internist, he suggested having a ready stash of candy bars in my purse. I knew that this was not the answer.

The beginning of my journey to health began at the age of fifty, when my dermatologist diagnosed me with Alopecia, an autoimmune condition that results in hair loss. He suggested shots of cortisone in my scalp, a remedy not guaranteed to work or to last. I walked out of his office determined to do research before resorting to his suggestion. Studying led me to learn about the connection between Alopecia and gluten. I asked my internist if I could be tested to see if gluten was at the root of my hunger and hair loss.

A few days after my tests were done, I received a letter stating that I had Celiac Disease and must go gluten free. I finally had an explanation for my lifelong unrelenting hunger, leg tremors, mood swings like nobody's business, Psoriasis, Osteopenia, Osteoporosis, and Alopecia, to be followed several years later by a diagnosis of Asthma and Raynaud's Syndrome.

My parents, my internist (the one who suggested eating candy bars), and my dermatologist only had my good health in mind. When I was a child, Celiac Disease was rare. It wouldn't have occurred to my parents to have my thin frame and constant hunger checked out by my pediatrician. Ask any doctor whether their studies included nutrition and they'll most likely tell you that they had an hour of it in all of their medical school training.

SMALL STEPS

So now what can you do? Take small steps, consult with your child's doctor, and talk to other parents whose children have gluten issues. There are many resources for helping you as your child's journey to health begins. While the first few months are the hardest, I can assure you that it will get easier in time. This may be the best thing that ever happened to your family's health!

Ellen is a Certified Holistic Health Coach who teaches people who are gluten free how to love the food that will love them back. She is also a multi-award-winning Children's Recording Artist, Performer, and Early Childhood Music Educator.

Gigi Gravel

Gigi Gravel, a Weight Loss Transformation and Empowerment Coach, is a graduate of the University of Denver with a BS in Environmental Science and Biology, a Certified Holistic Health Coach from the Institute of Integrative Nutrition, and a Certified Transformation Coach from Holistic MBA.

Gigi's innovative coaching style helps clients breakthrough the barriers that are undermining their weight loss efforts, empowering them with cutting-edge knowledge and effective strategies to boldly take charge of their diet, transform their body, mind, and spirit, and achieve successful and lasting weight loss so they can revitalize the exciting and vibrant life they desire and deserve.

🏠 www.GigiGravel.com

f www.facebook.com/gigi.gravel.1

f www.facebook.com/WeightLossTransformationCoach

LESSON 10

Hungry for Change: A Transformative and Empowering Approach to Weight Loss

By Gigi Gravel

~~~

My out-of-control eating and skyrocketing weight were not a reflection of a moment in time, but a story many years in the making—thirty-five to be exact! Thirty-five years of denial, fear, and rationalization; thirty-five years of stuffing my feelings, denying my feelings; and thirty-five years of denying who I was and not expressing how I felt. But it was those thirty-five years that helped me find my purpose in life and empowered me to overcome challenges and become the confident, vibrant woman I am today!

I don't know exactly what reason made me want to make changes in my life, but I did know I was tired of being overweight, unhealthy, and unhappy. Throughout my life, I battled with my weight and struggled unsuccessfully with endless diets that left me feeling defeated and depressed. Sadly, through all the discipline and deprivation, I ended up weighing a whopping 248 lbs., with low energy, high cholesterol, and a sluggish metabolism.

Below is an excerpt from a letter I wrote just three years ago:

"I sit here before you today because I am disgusted and at wits end with myself...I am compulsively eating and continually dieting... My out-of-control eating has already affected my mental wellbeing, as it consumes my every thought. I'm giving myself permission to stuff my face because I don't feel I have the inner strength to face one more failed weight loss attempt…I can't keep living my life this way, I deserve so much more…"

I didn't understand how I ended up in this seemingly endless funnel of pain, but I did know I was tired of living this way…and I was hungry for change!

I started examining how my thoughts and emotions were undermining my weight loss efforts and keeping me stuck repeating the same ineffective diet patterns. Searching for answers started me on an amazing transformation journey of self-discovery and personal growth. My weight loss challenge had become my gift and I was ready to share it with the world!

Through my education and decades of unsuccessful weight loss attempts, I finally discovered the secret to successful weight loss; and unfortunately, we're all missing it! We're not failing diets, diets are failing us! Weight loss is *not* about restricting "bad" foods or having iron-clad willpower, as diet gurus and society would have us believe.

Diets don't work! The results aren't positive because the approach is negative and self-defeating. Diets imply a short-term commitment where we make radical food changes until we reach our desired weight. They focus on the end result and how quickly we can achieve it, so we either fail or succeed. When we "fail" to meet the diet's unrealistic expectations, the voices in our heads start telling us we've "failed" because we're weak and we'll never get our eating under control and lose weight. These negative emotions quickly kick in what I call the four barriers to successful and lasting weight loss: fear, resistance, sabotage, and stress. These are diet killers! It's nearly impossible to successfully lose weight coming from this place of negativity and disempowerment.

After many years of failed weight loss attempts, we feel defeated, our confidence shattered, and we start doubting our abilities to take on any challenge and succeed. We feel depressed, frustrated, and angry so we eat to suppress and numb these negative feelings and predictably start the relentless diet cycle, until we finally throw in the towel and give up. Diets don't work!

To achieve lasting weight loss, we have to stop focusing on the diets themselves because chronic dieting and weight issues aren't problems;

they're symptoms of dis-ease, alerting us that something is wrong and out of balance in our lives. We need to listen! They're telling us that we need to change not only how we eat, but also how we think and live. Don't get me wrong, a healthy diet is certainly an important part of weight loss, but simply changing your diet is not the most effective way to achieve lasting results; change must come from within.

Weight loss isn't a quick fix or a wave of the wand but a magical journey of personal growth and self-discovery that requires three Levels of Transformation: mind, body, and spirit. It's a process of gaining confidence, finding strength, and getting empowered so we can sustainably lose weight, reclaim our health, and live the amazing life we deserve.

THE THREE LEVELS OF TRANSFORMATION & EMPOWERMENT

Level 1: Transformation of the Mind

Dieters are almost always disempowered at this level. Their many failed weight loss attempts manifest as negative self-talk as they continually tell themselves they'll never lose weight, they're not strong enough, and there must be something wrong with them. "I am a weight loss failure" becomes their story, and over time progresses to "I am a failure." These self-defeating thoughts dissuade them from taking on new challenges. If they do finally muster enough strength to make a move, resistance and sabotage will quickly emerge and derail their efforts. When we're disempowered at this level, it'll be nearly impossible to reach our ideal weight or maintain it for very long because we're coming from a place of negative thoughts and self-defeating beliefs.

To get empowered at this level, we need to dig deep and uncover the areas of our lives that are out of balance, driving us to eat uncontrollably, and blocking us from reaching our goals.

Transformation occurs when we're able to release negative thoughts and beliefs and create new ways of thinking that'll empower us to confidently take on any weight loss challenge and be victorious!

Level 2: Transformation of the Body

We're disempowered at this level because we lack knowledge of what's truly beneficial for our body and health. It's not our fault! There's lots of bad information and misrepresented facts out there, as the food industry appears to have placed money and power above our health.

To get empowered at this level, we need to acquire sound nutrition information and learn how to effectively shop for healthier products by learning how to decipher food labels and spot hidden toxic ingredients. We also need to discover how to prepare our kitchen, stock our pantry, and create delicious nutritious recipes the whole family will love.

Transformation at this level happens when we create a healthy relationship with foods that are right for our body. We realize weight loss isn't about restricting foods and cutting out our favorite treats but falling in love with nutritious foods and finding healthier solutions for our indulgences.

Level 3: Transformation of the Spirit

Chronic dieters consume themselves with food and dieting as protection from being exposed and the fear of revealing their true feelings. On the surface, they may appear to have it all together, but inside they're crumbling. They tend to lack self-esteem and don't truly believe, consciously or subconsciously, they're worthy of having what they really want, so they settle for what they have. They feel unclear and insecure about their creative intelligence and are more fearful of reaching their true potential than failing.

After transforming our mind and body, we're no longer burdened by our obsession with our diet and weight and are now empowered to tap into our creative genius, find our passion, discover our unique gifts, and creatively express ourselves.

We're transformed at this level when we've shifted our priorities from losing weight to loving ourselves and our lives. We're now inspired and motivated to reach the highest expression of ourselves, step into our genius, and share our gifts with the world. We're fully energized and empowered to boldly start a new chapter in our lives with total confidence and unbridled enthusiasm.

As you can see, weight loss is so much more than buying into "the less we eat, the more we lose" mentality. This approach may work short-term, but this self-defeating and ineffective strategy leads to frustration, stress, and anxiety, and we'll more than likely gain back all the lost weight and then some—losing a little piece of ourselves every time. In order to be successful and sustainable, weight loss needs to encompass the total person—mind, body, and spirit—and be approached as a transformational journey and empowering experience.

Unfortunately, if we as Moms are constantly on diets, battling with food, and struggling with our weight, there's a good chance the next generation will continue the pathology. Developing a healthy relationship with food and our bodies, and getting control of our weight, is important because our thoughts and actions are absorbed and imitated by our children. Letting go of negative thoughts and beliefs will foster an environment for letting in peace, joy, and happiness that'll not only affect our wellbeing but also our kids. We have the power within us to transform our mind, body, and spirit, take charge of our weight, reclaim our health, and create the life we desire and deserve. We just have to be hungry for change!

Lisa A. Rizzoli

Lisa A. Rizzoli is an Advanced Certified Tantra Educator, a Certified Spiritual Sexual Educator, and a Certified Divine Feminine Educator. She has taught with Charles Muir, the founder of Source School of Tantra. She completed her training with the Divine-Feminine Awakened Masculine Institute, Source School of Tantra Yoga, and Level 2 Ipsalu Tantra Kriya Yoga. Lisa leads monthly Puja ceremonies, facilitates workshops, and offers private sessions in Reno, NV. She continues to follow her path of Tantra study and Spiritual Education throughout the world.

✉ **info@tantrasacredloving.com**

⌂ **www.tantrasacredloving.com**

f **www.facebook.com/TantraSacredLovingWorkshops**

📞 **775 741 4090**

LESSON 11

A Busy Mom's Most Important Love Affair

By Lisa A. Rizzoli

~~~

</div>

Our lifetime is a series of love affairs that begin, end, overlap, multiply, and begin anew. As infants, we experience our first love affairs with our parents, and, in some cases, siblings. Growing into childhood, we find our next love affairs in the form of friendships with both real and sometimes imaginary people. Physical, sexual, and other dimensions shape the love affairs we have in our teen years and early 20s.

Busy moms, however, can be overwhelmed by the simultaneous love affairs that enrich their lives. Being a mother to one or more children, being a lover to a significant other, remaining a child to her parents, and sustaining friendships that transcend years, if not decades, takes a staggering amount of energy.

Few, if any women, can participate in that many love affairs—let alone savor them and thrive in them—if she fails to establish and nourish her most important love affair: the one she has with herself.

I have found no greater way to do that than the art of sacred loving, also called Tantra.

AN ACCIDENTALLY TANTRIC DELIVERY

I was nineteen years old and pregnant with my first child. I felt deeply connected and knew everything would be OK. Throughout my life, whenever I felt stressed, scared, or frightened, I knew God was with me and I would be OK.

Late in my third trimester, I found myself sitting with a friend on metal bleachers, watching my husband win a championship softball game. That is when the contractions began.

My friend was timing the contractions at ten minutes apart. She was nervous but I was not. Ten minutes is a long time and the contractions did not hurt. Labor was supposed to hurt, I thought.

My energy waned as the night wore on through the game and its celebration. I went to bed and slept through the night. The next day I had an appointment with my OB, who told me I was indeed in labor and that I needed to be induced.

At the hospital, the nurses were kind and supportive as they hooked me up to monitors and an I.V. The drugs they administered to me intensified my pain and sped up my contractions.

There was soon a conflict between what others were telling me and what my body was telling me. My nurses and sister urged me to breathe a certain way. I followed my body's wisdom, however, and breathed the way it wanted me to.

The drugs were too much and, thankfully, they agreed to remove them. That allowed my body to rediscover its natural rhythm. The intensity of the contractions lessened. I could rest between them.

The urge to push changed my breathing once again to manage the new stress. We rushed to the delivery room. They urged me to delay pushing. I knew that was impossible.

Finally, they told me it was okay to push. One push and my baby crowned. The doctor was not in the room yet and they were telling me to wait. How ridiculous, I thought, as if this was occurring on his or even my schedule.

With the doctor finally present, I took a deep breath, filling myself with Divine energy, and pushed again. My daughter's head emerged. The pain, now intense, shifted my breathing again, transforming the pain I felt into the exquisite pleasure.

An orgasm rocked through every inch of my body, though it was unlike any other orgasm I had ever felt. Every cell in my body was alive with this energy. I inhaled deeply and my brain was enveloped in feel-good chemicals, like oxytocin and endorphins.

My body called for me to bear down again and another wave of pleasure washed over me as the body of my daughter burst forth. The wave of force I felt filled me with pure bliss. Holding her gave me a deeper understanding of pure love.

UNDERSTANDING WHAT HAPPENED THAT DAY

Years later, I attended a workshop that introduced me to the philosophy of Tantra. The concepts of sacred sexuality and sexual healing were a springboard for me. I wanted to experience deeper and more intimate connections. I wanted to know about the incredible beauty and magic of my body, which included mythical-sounding wonders, like orgasmic variations and the difference between orgasm and ejaculation. I delved into the study of sexuality, communication, Shamanism, Neo-Tantra and classic Tantra, yoga, and the chakras.

The class focused on sexual techniques and concepts that simultaneously felt new and yet familiar. Learning—or was it re-learning?--these ideas made me yearn to know more about the depth and the breadth of the physical, mental, emotional, energetic, and spiritual consequences of who I am. From my efforts to study Tantra techniques, meditation, breath work, visualization, and the body's energetic chakras comes a deeper understanding that everything is connected and everything is sacred.

BRING TANTRA INTO YOUR LIFE TODAY

Working with a Certified Tantra Educator (CTE), attending workshops dedicated to Tantra, and even finding community with other tantric students are all wonderful things. None of them are necessary, however, to begin this sacred practice and reap its benefits.

Tantra is a spiritual practice that weaves all aspects of life—the physical, mental, emotional, energetic, and spiritual—into one. We can do any task mindlessly or we can choose to use all our senses to enhance our awareness and thoroughly enjoy the experience.

Tantra is a modality of seeing the ordinary as extraordinary and the extraordinary as ordinary, and finding the balance in our lives to see the sacred in all. Cultivating sexual energies brings us into our bodies, into the moment, to feel what it means to be alive, and to get our creative juices flowing.

A quick, easy technique to do is a Tantric pubococcygeus (PC) muscle exercise, also known as Kegel or pelvic floor exercises.

You can locate the pubococcygeus muscle by consciously stopping your urine flow. Once you identify your PC muscles, you can proceed.

- Begin by squeezing the PC as you inhale for the slow count of five, hold tight, tighter for a slow count of five. Slowly release the hold and the breath for a count of five until you reach neutral.

- With the breath held out slowly and gently, push out for a count of five and bring it back to neutral, and repeat 5 times.

- When first beginning this exercise, be gentle and kind to your body, as you are building muscle and could be sore if you do too many. I visualize an elevator rising up five floors, stopping at each floor, and then descending each floor and going into a deep basement.

Another simple exercise is to "pulse" on the PC muscle throughout the day. Squeeze, release, squeeze, release several times then hold and squeeze tightly while holding the breath, then slowly release the hold and the breath. Allow yourself to focus on the surge of energy that release creates.

Including the breath and visualizations enhances these exercises. You can make them as sexy as you wish through your intentions and awareness. Connecting and honoring the sacred space within you brings more energy and creativity into your life, fueling the love affair you must have with yourself in order to be your best for the many other love affairs that fills your life as a mom.

The beautiful thing about these is that once you have identified the muscle, you can do these exercises anywhere, anytime, and no one has to know what you are doing. Whenever you feel stress or anxiety, ride the elevator or pulse your PC muscle, and bring yourself into the place of calmness through feeling sexy with your own being.

These are incredible exercises to do with your partner as well. I invite you to give your partner a ride on your amazing elevator.

NOURISH YOUR SELF-LOVE AFFAIR

Tantra is a spiritual path that teaches us how to live in this world and be spiritual. It allows us to sustain the countless love affairs that make our life special by nourishing the vital love affair we must have with ourselves.

Some spiritual practices emphasize the concept of non-attachment and seek to separate the physical and the spiritual to allow one to better relate to the Divine. Tantra is different. It seeks to unite one's physical and spiritual natures in order to better connect with God. For example, doing laundry can become a meditation.

Tantra sees the body as a living temple. Tantra is a way of being and feeling. By cultivating and nurturing our creative life-force energies, our sexual energies, we open our souls. That, in turn, enriches how we experience our lives and deepens our ability to love.

The love affairs of being a mother and a grandmother have been the most rewarding, challenging, and spiritual experiences of my life. Without a foundation in Tantra, without the love affair I enjoy with myself, I may well have missed many things in the business of life.

Angie Topbas

Angie Topbas, Certified Holistic Health Coach and American Association of Drugless Practitioners member, inspires busy moms who aspire to lead a healthier and happier life. Angie is a graduate of the Institute for Integrative Nutrition and a mom. She received her MBA from Thunderbird in 2001, and she has a BA in Business Administration.

Angie, through her individual and group health coaching programs, supports moms around setting and measuring health and lifestyle goals, teaches how to make healthier choices at grocery stores and restaurants, and guides on preparing quick, easy, healthy but tasty meals and snacks for the whole family.

✉ angie@lusciousnutritious.com

✉ angie.topbas@gmail.com

🏠 www.lusciousnutritious.com

🏠 www.balanceforbusymoms.com

f www.facebook.com/lusciousnutritious

f www.facebook.com/AngieTopbas

🐦 www.twitter.com/AngieTopbas

in www.linkedin.com/pub/angie-enci-topbas/0/404/a37

- www.instagram.com/AngieTopbas
- 212 300 5785
- Skype: encitopbas75

LESSON 12

Discovering Your Inner Health Coach

By Angie Topbas

~~~

My journey started with a deep passion to do something totally different, and a coincidence that followed. My seven-year-old daughter at the time had just turned three. I had been a stay-at-home mom for three years. Most stay-at-home moms agree that after a few years of going on play dates and participating in activities, you start questioning your life with questions like, "What about my career? How can I contribute to our income? Should I go back to work?" For me, when these questions came up, I only knew one thing for sure… I did not want to go back to the corporate world. However, I also couldn't figure out my true purpose. One thing I knew for sure was I really enjoyed helping people; and when I helped someone (i.e., helping an elder cross the street), I felt my happiest.

When a friend suggested that I check out Institute for Integrative Nutrition (IIN), little did I know my life would change forever. I also had no clue that I would be able to heal myself from a condition that I had suffered from for almost twenty years. When I turned seventeen, I was diagnosed with GERD—severe acid reflux/gastritis—and prescribed medication. I was dependent on these pills until age thirty-four. I would experience intense burning, starting from my stomach to my throat, if I forgot to take my pill one day. So, I never missed a pill for seventeen years. Of course, the side effects and long-term damage of these pills were never explained.

During my training in Holistic Health at IIN, I learned much about healing foods, like dark leafy greens, and bio-individuality (one person's food can be another person's poison); and I started experimenting with new foods and ingredients. I incorporated green smoothies into my diet and ate more alkalinizing foods. I discovered the foods I was sensitive to, removed those from my diet, and searched for alternatives. Adding probiotics, digestive enzymes, using chopsticks, chewing each bite at least thirty times, and drinking water before meals and at least one hour after meals were some of the other practices that I incorporated. Within three months, I was able to eliminate my medication completely. Today, I know what does and doesn't work for my body without needing any hair tests or blood work to figure it out.

My story is just one simple example highlighting that we all have a health coach inside us, and we all can become our own health coach. However, some of you may not be patient enough to go through the process alone, or know how to begin the process. This is when the support of a health coach, who guides you through the challenges and ensures that you reach your health and lifestyle goals, will be of great benefit. Please remember though, change doesn't happen overnight, and patience is key. Whether it is rebalancing your life or making diet and lifestyle improvements for the family, be aware transformation happens once you start introducing healthy habits to your routine and maintain them long-term. Working with moms, I find that health, movement, cooking, home environment, friendships, and social life are some of the most important elements, other than food, that feed their mind, body, and spirit.

Most of us take health for granted. We don't realize that having functioning bodies and being able to keep daily activities is actually a gift, until something major happens to a loved one or to us. Two years ago, I injured both of my shoulders during an intense yoga program. I wasn't able to drive for three months. I couldn't raise my arms to store the dishes. To this day, I still suffer. When we lose our ability to do things we take for granted, we realize that nothing really matters without good health. However, it doesn't always have to be this way. You and only you are in charge of your health. So, start making your health a priority by not missing your annual physical appointments, feeding your body whole foods, drinking more water, sleeping well, reducing/quitting caffeine, sugar, alcohol, and tobacco, moving your body in a way that you enjoy, and listening to your body and what it is trying to tell you.

By now, we all know that exercise is essential for optimal health. Similar to a child who tries to release his energy by running around, moms also need to move their bodies in a loving way. When I work with clients, rather than telling them to go to the gym, I encourage them to figure out the type of movements that nourish not only their bodies but also their minds and souls. Personally, I get bored with routine. So over the last couple of years, I've tried Pilates, yoga, Zumba, ballet, walking/running, and strength training. Each of these activities has impacted my life at a different level. Yoga made me feel more spiritual, while ballet made me feel like a performing artist. Recently, I tried a home-based exercise, an exercise trampoline…needless to say, it became very popular with both my daughter and husband. Once you discover what you really enjoy and start seeing the physical and psychological benefits, exercise becomes a joy and part of life that is indispensable rather than another chore.

Eating home-cooked foods is one of the most important factors in becoming a healthier and happier person. If you are a full-time working parent, planning becomes crucial. It might be challenging for you to spend time in the kitchen during the week. So try cooking in bulk on a Sunday afternoon and consume that meal in different ways during the week. For example, you can serve cooked brown rice as breakfast porridge with almond milk, nuts, and seeds, or as dinner with animal protein and vegetables. Please remember you don't always have to cook fancy meals. Make your meals simple, with few ingredients, and once in a while, if you're into it, follow a more complicated recipe and prepare a gourmet meal. Light candles and turn cooking into a meditative process. It's also important to involve your children. Despite a potential mess, they'll enjoy experimenting with food and you'll appreciate the laughs and smiles shared together. Don't forget that when you prepare healthy meals/snacks for yourself and family, your body will thank you big time by having more energy. In turn, it will make you a more health-conscious and effective mom.

Home environment is another crucial part of overall wellbeing, often overlooked by busy moms. Having children at home adds more disorganization at home. If you find yourself overwhelmed with excess stuff, it's time to clean up. I had a client who was concerned about the chaos of her children's playroom. During a session, we decided she would prioritize this project. Once she took the initiative and felt accountable, she re-organized the playroom, and two weeks later, she looked extremely happy and relieved. Some tips to get started: Organize a few drawers at a time, rather than overwhelming yourself with the whole house. Get two garbage bags. Use one for items you'd like to donate, and one for things you'll throw away. Involve your children in the process, asking what they'd like to keep/discard. Check out this app, "Artkive," that helps to archive your children's drawings, artwork, homework, etc. Do the happy dance when you're done! As clutter disappears, you'll find that you've created more space for new things and opportunities to enter your life.

I'll never forget what the founder of IIN, Joshua Rosenthal, said during one of his classes about relationships. "No matter how much broccoli you eat, if you don't have healthy relationships, you won't be living your life at full capacity." Friendships and social life nourish you, playing a critical role in your health and happiness. Take time to evaluate your relationships and decide who supports your dreams and goals. Spend more time with friends who lift you up and make you laugh, and less time with people who drag you down. Make time to call and meet with a friend. If you get carried away in your own family issues, share your feelings with friends. Most of the time, you'll find that others are where you are or in worse conditions. Hearing other stories helps put things into perspective. In November 2013, my father passed away after tremendous physical and emotional pain during his last few months. My mom and I witnessed his suffering very closely. Every time I talk to my mom, she mentions that her friendships and social life have been instrumental in dealing with the recovery of losing her life partner.

I wanted to give you a glimpse of how easy it is to discover your inner health coach, which we all have inside. If you need a helping hand, I am here for you. In the meantime, start by seeing your health as your most valuable asset, and take action to improve it. Find out what kind of movement brings you joy. Prioritize to eat home-cooked foods. Organize your home in a way that brings you peace of mind, and spend more time with friends who bring out the best in you! The rest will come, I PROMISE…

Sonja M. Ramos

Sonja Ramos is a Branding and Visibility Coach serving conscious women entrepreneurs in the healing arts.

Sonja has a degree in Outdoor Education from the University of Minnesota Duluth and has worked for Outward Bound and other outdoor education providers. She has a deep love for nature and loves to venture outdoors for all types of adventures. She is also a Certified Hatha Yoga teacher, a Certified Holistic Health Coach through IIN, and a Massage Therapist. Sonja gets all the inspiration for her work with clients worldwide through her connection to nature and spirit.

🏠 www.sonjaramos.com

f www.facebook.com/freshbettylifestyle

🐦 www.twitter.com/thefreshbetty

🅿 www.pinterest.com/freshbetty

Life Beyond Yoga Pants: Embrace Your Unique Style and Beauty and Let it Shine!

By Sonja M. Ramos

I'm going to describe a ridiculously familiar scenario and I would love to know if you relate! Let me indulge you:

It's 7:55 a.m. and the school bus is scheduled to arrive in five minutes! Everyone is scrambling and clawing for backpacks, missing hats, mittens, and probably a permission slip that should have been turned in yesterday. Voices are rising, the dog is whining, and your blood pressure is bursting! You finally get out the door and begin making your way to the bus, only to see it pull away from the curb.

Now you have to get everyone loaded in the car and drive to school. This means you'll probably see some people you know. You glance in the rearview mirror and realize you've neither brushed your hair nor washed your face. You also realize that you grabbed the first available pants that you found on the floor, because the baskets of unfolded clothes from three days ago were in total chaos, and since it was dark in the first place, those yoga pants looked like a trusty friend, and besides, they are SO COMFORTABLE. You have no bra on and the tee shirt you grabbed to wear under that sweatshirt is questionably clean, because it was lying in a heap on the bed.

As you get to the car, you notice the empty Starbucks cups littering and rolling around on top of the papers and other clutter on the floor of the passenger side.

"OMG," you think, and then another thought flashes into your mind. One that speaks, "I am NOT available for this anymore!"Does any of this scene sound familiar to you? It sure does to me! I have BEEN that mom more times than I can tell you! Let me also be transparent here, too—I still am sometimes, but not NEARLY as much as I used to be.

I now have a morning routine that has been a lifesaver, and I call it my Blissipline routine. It has really helped me get grounded, centered, and more connected with my body, my femininity, and my family. Having a routine that is set and orderly can hold you in a space of stability and calm, and you wake up every day with intention, instead of just going through the motions on autopilot and letting yourself sweat the small stuff. When you have Blissipline holding you every morning as you start your day, you feel calm, centered, and in control, which you ARE. You also feel inclined to bring out your true beauty and not let it be suppressed. You actually WANT to brush your hair, wash your face, and pick out some nice clothes that are totally YOUR style. You FEEL good and in turn, you LOOK good naturally because you radiate a feeling of wellbeing and calm, and that is VERY SEXY.

When the other family members get up for the day, you greet them with love. The whole morning unfolds peacefully and orderly, and you find that there is PLENTY of time to pack lunches, get back packs ready, put clean clothes on, wash your face, brush your hair, and have a nice leisurely walk to the bus. Doesn't that sound better than the former description? How can you bring this into YOUR life?

It all starts with a decision. Making a definite decision that you are just not available for allowing stress and chaos into your daily routine anymore is the number one step you must take if you want to enter into a life beyond yoga pants! If you want to enter into each day with calm and balance and time for YOU. If you want to let your beauty and femininity shine outward, instead of feeling dull, frumpy, and exhausted, wearing old tee shirts and yoga pants as your main uniform. Yes, you will probably have to get up earlier than everyone else, and yes, you may have to shove your ego aside and ask for some help, but I promise you, it will be SO worth it in the long run! Everyone wins too, not just you. The entire house feels the benefit of this one little change that you will make initially for YOURSELF. When you start feeling more balanced and calm, a ripple effect is created that reaches all those around you and it is beautiful!

Let's talk about the beauty factor for minute. I'm not talking model or celebrity beauty, but your TRUE beauty. Have you let it slip away? Have you allowed it to diminish for some reason? Do you not take care of yourself the way you once did because life has gotten so busy that taking half an hour to an hour for yourself to enjoy a luxurious bubble bath and then rubbing your favorite lotion all over your skin seems like too much effort? I have been there and back again, my friend! I also know that if I don't take a little time for myself to enjoy something like a bath, or even 15 minutes of yoga, by myself, or a walk in the fresh air, I feel depleted, exhausted, diminished. Not only do I feel it in my heart, but I see it in my face in the mirror, and I can also see it in my body. My skin looks dull, my eyes don't sparkle, my hair looks dull and unkempt. In other words, BLAH.

When I am in alignment though, and in my groove of commitment to myself, I radiate beauty! As I write this, I am five months pregnant and I look radiant! I have two other children that I had at a much younger age, and because I am much more connected to my body and myself, I also have a firm commitment to take time for myself. I look better now at forty-one than I did at twenty-nine when I had my first baby! I let my beauty shine out, too. I brush my hair and celebrate my mane, instead of always putting it up or in a ponytail, like I used to. I wash and moisturize my face twice daily, and I wear makeup that is all natural and enhances my glow. I feel fantastic, and as a result of that feeling fantastic, it shows on the outside. When I feel fantastic, I am naturally joyful, loving, and giving and in turn, I receive that back! Let your beauty come through you. Wear the clothes that look great on your body, wear colors that bring out the colors in your eyes and skin tone, adorn yourself with jewels, gold, and silver. You are a GODDESS, and everyone should know that!

So, how to bring this Blissipline that is a game changer into your life? In the first few weeks of doing this, it might be a good idea to get an accountability buddy or partner to do this with you. When I started doing this, I had a group of girlfriends who were going through similar patterns, and we decided to do it together and hold each other accountable. It is really easy to say you will do this and maybe do it for a few days or a week but then let old habits take over. Find a trusted friend who is like-minded and you can help each other out. I would also get a journal and begin journaling each morning.

Start by going to bed each night with an intention of how you will start your day the next morning. When morning comes and that alarm rings, remember the intention that you set the night before, and it should pull you out of bed. Once you are up, take some time to sit quietly, and if you meditate or have a prayer practice, this is a perfect time to give thanks for this beautiful new day and all the possibilities of today and also having gratitude for all that you have around you right now. Take a few more minutes to visualize how you would like your day to be, and take yourself to that space and allow yourself to feel that day unfolding and all of the good things that will happen and how you'll have an abundance of time! Next, you could do a little yoga or stretching and then spend some time journaling about yesterday and today and what you are grateful for each day. Then, enjoy the silence! Make coffee or tea and see the light come into the sky and notice how beautiful everything is. As you hear rustling coming from the rooms upstairs, or down the hall, you are ready and excited to greet your amazing family as they rise for the day!

Remember, Rome was NOT built in a day and these things take time. Be gentle with yourself and stay committed to YOU!

Sarah Mastriani-Levi

Sarah Mastriani-Levi, creator of Mannafest Living, serves as an International Holistic Health Coach and Personal Chef. She is often referred to as a boldly authentic spiritual pioneer, creative visionary, and inspirational catalyst. She lectures internationally and offers workshops and holistic health coaching for the health-curious to the avidly health-conscious.

Parallel to her holistic consulting and various food services, she actively homeschools her four children, as a single-parent, raising them with a strong bond to nature. She has raised them in an ecological manner, in harmony with nature. Her children have grown from all of the fresh goodness nature has to offer, both physically and spiritually.

- contact@mannafest-living.com
- www.mannafest-living.com
- www.facebook.com/organic.veggie.girl
- www.facebook.com/MannafestLiving
- www.twitter.com/mannafestliving
- www.pinterest.com/MannafestLiving/
- www.linkedin.com/pub/sarah-mastriani-levi/66/430/7a1
- Skype: organic_veggie_girl

LESSON 14

Embrace Your Child's Natural Rhythm through Organic Gardening

By Sarah Mastriani-Levi

~~~

Moms are curious how to slow down when everything around them is telling them that there are not enough hours in the day. If we are willing to listen, nature offers many important lessons in slowing down.

When my first babies (twins) were ready to begin supplementing their breast-feeding with solid food, I became concerned with purity of what I would feed them. I wanted only organic fresh fruits and vegetables, and my (then) husband felt that organic was a monetary heist without much proof of its "organicness." We were living in Israel, where the market for organic food was less strictly supervised than in many Western countries. He was the breadwinner…so my argument fell on deaf ears. I had to think outside the box. That's it, I'd grow my own, but that would take a long time. Regardless, I knew that I'd have to start somewhere. There were two clear options that seemed fairly dependable: seedlings from an organic supplier, or organic seeds. When I approached the seedling supplier, he said that I'd have to buy trays (one hundred seedlings of each thing that I wanted to grow). That wouldn't work with my small garden and the cost of the trays…so seeds became the only viable option. There was only one problem—I had never grown organic vegetables before. However, I was bound and determined to give my kids the best nutrition that I could, without rocking the financial "boat" on the home front. I read organic gardening books, studied the internet, and visited friends who were growing practically anything, to try to understand how they were doing what they were doing. Suddenly, I started to notice that the more the babies and I walked around in people's gardens, the calmer they became. Determined not to get stuck in analysis-paralysis, I made a personal agreement that I wouldn't beat myself up if I didn't get it exactly right, and that I should just jump in. I bought some organic compost and soil and started some seeds in little plastic containers I had in my recycling bin. Just being willing to try created a shift in perception and opened my heart to begin receiving more blessings than I could ever imagine.

WHY GROW ORGANIC?

It's OK. I hear those gears inside your head saying:

- "Why should I grow my own organic food when nearly everything is available in the supermarket?"

and

- "Who has time for all of that nonsense?"

I'd agree, but I noticed some side effects that were worth paying attention to.

The most important was the understanding of "a process" and how long a process takes. I remember having an in-depth conversation with a brilliant friend about going through a spiritual process. She looked at me and said, "How long does it usually take you until the opaqueness abates?" I stammered and realized that in spite of the fact I was on a spiritual path, I just really didn't know how long it took me to gain clarity. I turned that question over in my mind for a very long time. As I began digging my fingers into the soil and creating small gardens, I realized gardens weren't for me. Yeah, I know it sounds counter-intuitive, but I realized that my gardens were for my children...for the world. It seems lofty, but suddenly as I looked at the seedlings, I understood that each of those seedlings were like people that I had encountered in life. They were all going through a process. They became a metaphor for everything that I wanted and didn't want to see in others. The gardens no longer represented just sustenance, but rather an understanding of others' processes. No seedling was identical. Its survival was not guaranteed. Some plants developed slowly and became enormously fruitful. Other vigorous growers turned into stunted examples of root-locked decline. None of those plants read the books on their "ideal" growth patterns.

GROW YOUR OWN FOOD TO CREATE NATURAL RHYTHM

I was curious to understand spiritual and developmental processes. The universe stepped up and gave me many tangible examples. I just had to open my eyes and there they were. I developed a level of acceptance and dropped a level of expectation.

Just as the plants weren't aware of the developmental patterns that were "expected" of them on the seed packets, likewise, my children hadn't read the government's developmental growth curves. Yet, both were innately thriving—without asking permission or knowing "the process" that was expected of them. By growing various plants, I began to see individuality and to develop a respect for each plant and its offerings. The moment that I relinquished the idea that I had some control, I could see the gifts and the natural rhythm.

THE GIFTS OF ACCEPTANCE AND INTEGRATION

Nearly every gardener encounters visitors in the garden, especially organic gardeners. Part of the commitment to having an organic garden is the understanding that the chemicals used in conventional gardening techniques kill the big animals (us) slowly, just as they kill the tiny animals quickly. Having visitors (often called "unwanted pests") is part of the process. But what is one to do when all of the Swiss chard plants are suddenly covered in snails? I read about solutions at length (i.e., sinking cups filled with beer to the surface level and spraying leaves with vegetable-soaps), but all of those "solutions" seemed to have one thing in common—killing or deterring the imposters. Within myself, I couldn't make peace with it. I began to realize that the snails needed to eat too, and that perhaps the approach I had used until then was skewed. I made a decision to allow the snails to remain in the garden. Moreover, I decided that I would create a special place in the garden and designate it "the snail home." I chose a bush that would be just for the snails. I plucked off a lot of them from the chard plants and transferred them to the bush. Each time I would say to them,

"You are welcomed in my garden. Here is a place especially for you." I know this sounds really hokey, but the strangest thing happened. If I hadn't experienced it myself, I'm not sure that I would believe it. Suddenly, **all** of the snails in the garden migrated to the "snail bush," and they were no longer eating my crops. The ecosystem of the home is so similar. When we choose to embrace all of what everyone brings to the table, instead of trying to remove the things that we think are "bad," everything can begin to thrive. Everyone finds their natural place and rhythm.

BECOME A GARDENING BAD-ASS—JUST START!

Starting a small garden doesn't have to be a massive undertaking to be effective, both for the plants and the spiritual process that often ensues. There are many different options for setting up small gardens, and none of them is better than the other. It's possible to start small and still enjoy this activity. My one initial bit of advice would be: grow something that you love to eat.

Plants have few requirements: water, light, air, and love.

- A simple herb garden can be started in the smallest of spaces, even on a windowsill in an apartment. I would recommend buying herbs that are already plants, rather than seeds, when first starting out. This will enable you to begin enjoying them right away.

- Pots are a natural transition from an indoor herb garden and a fairly low investment to spread the goodness outdoors to your porch, balcony, or patio. In the winter, if your climate permits, grow leafy veggies in pots. Grow edible flowers too, like nasturtiums or pansies. In the summer, you can plant tomatoes and basil together, or flowering pole beans, and add a trellis for them to climb.

- Beds are slightly more labor intensive but allow you to grow more. They require observation and proper watering to thrive.

REFLECTIONS FROM THE MOUTHS OF BABES

I asked my children what growing up in the gardens taught them. Here are the lessons that nature had to offer:

- "You never get something by doing nothing. If you want something, you must be willing to work for it."

- "You must be present every day, just show up and observe."

- "You are responsible for everything that you do."

- "Everything takes time and has a pace of its own. Understanding that can teach patience and acceptance of others and situations."

For me, hearing my children say those words was authentic reassurance that the glorious rhythm of nature had spoken through its natural gifts. I was just lucky enough to witness it.

Go grow something…anything! Get your children involved. Allow them to observe the process. They will learn so much more than you alone could explain to them.

Nicole Eastman

Dr. Nicole Eastman is a bestselling, internationally published author who turned to therapeutic writing and ministry following a near-fatal car accident in December 2010. Prior to her accident, she earned her bachelor of science in psychology from Wayne State University and her degree in medicine from Michigan State University College of Osteopathic Medicine. Throughout her undergraduate studies she worked many jobs, including employment as a NASM and ACE certified personal trainer and AFAA certified group fitness instructor. Currently, Dr. Eastman resides in Grand Cayman with her husband, Tim, and their beautiful son, Jack.

✉ nicolemeastman1@gmail.com

⌂ www.drnicolemeastman.com

f www.facebook.com/pages/Dr-Nicole-M-Eastman-DO/226755637390614?ref=hl

f www.facebook.com/pages/Motor-Vehicle-Accident-Survivors/289911374379121?ref=hl

f www.facebook.com/BrainInjuryAwarenessMonth?ref=hl

🐦 www.twitter.com/DrNicoleEastman

in www.linkedin.com/pub/dr-nicole-eastman-d-o/36/b5/a8a/

Ⓢ Skype: timnicoleeastman

Location: Grand Cayman, Cayman Islands

LESSON 15

Finding Peace and Balance Despite Pain

By Nicole Eastman, D.O.

~~~

Tiny handprints on the sliding glass door, water thrown out of the tub when my attention momentarily diverts elsewhere, a little naked bum running with exuberant freedom, the occasional consequence of being one year old, male, and nude—the yellow, projectile stream making its way onto the tile floor, adding just a bit more excitement to the day of a growing boy, and little hands closing my computer as I try to capture my thoughts during a moment of clarity—welcome to my life. Welcome to my "imperfectly perfect" life.

As I reflect on life, I cannot help but revisit 2008. I was consumed with work and the mindset that I was too busy for a family. Maybe it wasn't the fact that I was working eighty hours per week that kept me from desiring to build a family but rather, the hurt of losing my fifty-three-year-old father quite suddenly to a stroke. I was twenty-six years old when I had to say goodbye to the strongest man in my life. With that, why would I want to allow myself to be vulnerable, to fall in love, to start a family, and then have it torn apart by loss—just as I witnessed happen in the family that was immediate to me growing up? No, thank you. I would pass. The masculine energy that I was raised with filled my soul, and walls were constructed in efforts to prevent any sort of vulnerability and potential hurt. Work and a highly social lifestyle took over.

Then, however, fate interceded, and in 2009, I met the man who would become my husband the following year. Then two weeks following our holy matrimony, a near-fatal accident nearly took my life. The realities of this accident, which was beyond my control, left me broken. Walls were demolished, emotions were visible, and I was left feeling alone. In this time of despair, I came to accept my faith in Christ; and, this allowed me to move forward with hope. I lost so much. However, I gained the insight that there was still purpose for my life. I suffered immensely as I sought out who "I" was, and the first place I received comfort was in knowing that I was a child of God.

Following acceptance of faith, I started to desire childbearing; but was this possible? I was on narcotic pain management, I experienced permanent spinal damage, which failed to be corrected through surgery, and I spent over seven months of the year in bed due to pain and fatigue. I did not have a good quality of life, so how could I possibly be a "perfect" mother?

There is no way to be a perfect mother, and a million ways to be a good one.

– Jill Churchill

Now, here is a little timeline to bring you up to date:

March 2012, Niagara Falls, Canada—New life conceived!

April 2012—Positive pregnancy test! My deepest subconscious desire was gifted to me; and now, I had even more reason to keep moving forward, despite the pain.

August 2012—My husband and I moved out of the country! Nearing the third trimester of pregnancy, we felt led to move to Grand Cayman. Third trimester, Grand Cayman, hottest months of the year, my husband turning off the air conditioning to save the little money we had—less than ideal for a Mom-in-the-making.

December 12, 2012—In labor! Holy painful contractions!

December 13, 2012—After about sixty-five pounds gained, very limited mobility due to too many potatoes, chocolate pudding, and a spine that appears to be many generations older than my chronological age, countless hours spent in the sea, overall, a "healthy" pregnancy, and hours of labor, our son went into fetal distress and had to be delivered via emergency cesarean section. To make matters worse, I could feel them cutting me, so I had to be intubated. When I awoke from the anesthesia, all I wanted to know was whether or not my baby was healthy, and thankfully, he was. My prayers for a healthy baby were answered. I hope to always remember the moment when I first saw Jack's face. He was my perfect miracle and tears of overwhelming gratitude streamed down my face.

Children are a gift from the Lord; they are a reward from him.

– Psalm 127:3

2013—An amazing year that went way too fast. Life contained many stressors, including the continuation of physical and psychological health issues, the added stress of being new parents while away from extended family, financial stress relating to disability, cultural stress related to our move, transitional stress relating to my husband's ADHD and narcolepsy and the addition of a newborn baby, stress relating to medical-legal issues, and stress relating to new opportunities for personal and professional growth.

So, with that all said, how have I balanced it all—the loss, the pain, the international relocation, my marriage, the needs of my husband, the needs of my son, MY needs? How have I come to find peace that surpasses all understanding?

Here is how:

- Fully Accepting Faith: God is at the center of my life, I believe in the power of prayer, and I accept that life is like a mist, so I live for each moment, recognizing that we never know when it will be our last. Life will continue to bring disappointments and unfavorable life circumstances. However, this ultimately serves to strengthen our faith. I believe that no matter what life brings, we have a loving God who works to bring healing and good to all who believe in Him.

- Embracing Positivity: The mind is powerful! Through rehearsal of positive affirmations and biblical scripture, I have come to embody truths, including, "I can do all things through Christ who strengthens me." (Philippians 4:13) Embracing positivity also means distancing myself from negativity. That means that I do not participate in "Mommy Wars," I shy away from watching the news, and I have distaste for gossip. As a woman and a Mom, I think it is time that we start building one another up. Here, I'll start: You are beautiful, you are doing your very best, you are more worthy than you realize, and you are loved.

- Expressing Gratitude: I am so thankful for this second chance at life. The more I focus on what I have to be thankful for, the less I focus on that which has previously weighed me down. I am thankful for love, forgiveness, "good days," reuniting with family, butterflies, sandy beaches, the peace that I receive when I am present with water, full-belly giggles, and warm cuddles…what are you thankful for? Take a moment to write a list of some of the many blessings in your life and place it where you get ready every morning. Leave room to add to your list and watch your list grow.

- Addressing Needs: Part of my journey has been acceptance that I am not Superwoman. I need rest, alone time, and quiet time. I need to express my emotions. I need to say "No." I need to know when to ask for and accept help. It is okay to ask for help! Paying attention to my own needs has allowed me to be more present and effective when I am taking care of the needs of others. What are your needs?

- Becoming Flexible: I have learned to go with the flow, to let go, and to accept life as it presents itself. This means that I no longer sweat the small stuff and I no longer need "perfection." It is okay to color outside the lines! It is okay to step out of comfort zones and to embrace uncertainty. It is okay to be forgiving to yourself.

Celebrating Motherhood: Motherhood has truly been the greatest gift of healing. It amazes me to think that there was a time in life that I thought that I didn't want this. To think of all of the joy and beauty that I would have missed out on had I allowed fear to prevent me from falling in love, to getting married, to becoming blessed with a baby. Never in a million years would I have envisioned myself as the mother that I am today—a mother who has found confidence and feminine expression through breastfeeding and attachment parenting, who "holds her son too much," "spoils him" with love, eye contact, and an abundance of smiles, who is drawn to women who are pregnant to tell them how beautiful they are and how much their life is going to change, but for the better! To think that God trusted me THAT much—allowing me to oversee the life of one of His children. That is a beautiful honor worth all of the sacrifice, isn't it? Take this moment to celebrate your life and your gift of motherhood. Celebrate the lessons you have learned along the way and moments made into memories, which you can treasure forever.

Julie Schuetz

Julie Schuetz is an award winning entrepreneur and philanthropist who passionately teaches that you are never too young or too old to pursue a dream and make it happen. As a certified health coach and co-owner of a dance studio, Julie is blessed to be able to empower girls and women of all ages to lead a healthy, fulfilled life while keeping those you love front and center. She is an expert in creating successful family businesses. Regardless of certifications and awards, the titles she holds with the most honor are wife, mom, mother-in-law, and grandmother.

✉ jlschuetz@aol.com

🏠 www.julieschuetz.com

🏠 www.kansascityhealthcoach.com

f www.facebook.com/julie.m.schuetz

f www.facebook.com/KansasCityHealthCoach

🐦 www.twitter.com/JulieLSchutez

LESSON 16

Unplug to Plug In

By Julie Schuetz

~~~

So many people rush through their days, their weeks, their months, their years, and in a flash, their family has grown and moved away, sometimes physically, but also emotionally. While it may seem this happened overnight, in fact, it was decades, a child's lifetime in the making.

Today we celebrate busy. It is the immediate response when asked, "How are you?" "Busy!" It rolls off the tongue without thought. Is all the busyness truly necessary? Are we creating a self-fulfilling prophesy by constantly speaking of how busy we are? While technology has been a blessing in many ways, it has become a tremendous curse with many families. Communication has ceased to exist in ways that past generations enjoyed.

People think the days of sitting on the front porch in a rocking chair or swing and discussing the day is a by-gone era and not realistic in today's 24/7 hurry up society. Actually, it is more attainable than one might realize. There are many "front porch" opportunities in each day, if we just become aware of them and use them to our advantage.

We are a zombie culture addicted to our electronic devices. Babies by a year old can open a cell phone and scroll apps. They hurry to pick up a phone left on a table and take it to the owner. Elementary school children believe a cell phone is a necessity. Facebook absorbs our waking hours. The virtual world has become our main world. Let's take a step back and examine what communication is really important and how we can spend more of our time on meaningful conversations with true loved ones and less on what we have been programmed in recent years to believe is important. The solution is two-fold. First, taking time to have real conversations, and second, being vigilant with the words we speak to and about our loved ones to create a family that is plugged into each other and truly enjoys being together.

Do you know your child's school schedule? Do you know who they sit next to in class? What did they have for lunch today? What are their favorite songs? Do you know the names of the kids on your child's team? When they look up at you in the stands, are you watching them, or are you reading a book or talking on your phone?

How about these: Do you know what your Facebook friend that you've never met had for dinner? Do you know what MLM company your virtual friends are promoting? Do you know the names of all the members of a reality TV show? Do you cheer on professional athletes that you do not know personally and become aggravated if you are interrupted watching them?

I'm not here saying there is anything wrong with being a sports fan or watching some TV. However, are you giving equal time and attention to those that truly matter? Are you pushing away the people that would be grief-stricken if something tragic happened to you? Are you putting your attention and energy towards those who your passing would only be a momentary thought, or they do not even know you exist?

Where to start? Well, rest assured I am not going to tell you to get up earlier or put something else on your never ending to do list. Simply make a few changes to the things you are already doing.

Moms spend time every day shuffling kids to school, sports, activities, play dates, you name it. This is one of the best times in the day to talk. To really connect, you must declare your car a tech-free zone. This means except for the car radio, which can be a shared singing experience, no phones, no computers, and certainly no mindless DVD player. I guarantee you that if you stick with this plan, you will be amazed how much your kids will share with you about what is going on with their lives. They will notice their community, learn directions, enjoy nature, and best of all, they will know that you know and really care about what is happening in their lives. I loved being in the car with my kids and hearing about their days. There is something about the safety of being together in the car away from others and not having to look directly at a parent, whose eyes are on the road, that lets children and even adults share in a way that is less intimidating than having to look at them and see all the reactions. I loved car trips as a kid because of the intimate time with my parents and siblings. Conversations, car games, singing songs, and even the silence while being together, are treasured memories. Memories I was certain to recreate with my husband and children. I knew my kids had found the same valuable experience when, as young teens, they asked us if instead of flying on our next vacation as we always had in the past, if we could please take a driving trip, because it would be even more fun. So, we packed the car, headed west for two weeks, and had the time of our lives. Memories that would not have been the same if everyone had their face and attention buried in their own virtual world. If you have been using the DVD player as a babysitter in your vehicle, I challenge you to reconsider and imagine all the fantastic conversations you are missing with your loved ones. You are all already together; please make the most of it.

The family dinner table is being lost, and along with it, family cohesiveness. As a certified health coach, I am a strong proponent of eating healthy; however, I believe just as strongly that regardless of what you are eating, sitting down and eating together is crucial to your health and happiness. If your dinner table is one of chaos and tension, your food, regardless of its nutritional value, will not digest as efficiently in your body. Be the catalyst to change the routine and make dinner a time everyone looks forward to. Serve something everyone loves. Start the conversation. Tell stories about when you were little or something funny you read or heard. Remember, even if seems like it, you are not the waiter or school lunch monitor, you are a cherished mom and your family loves to have you sit with them at the table, happy, laughing, and sharing stories. Your example of how to enjoy each other's company at mealtime will radiate through them in no time and dinner will go from stress to bliss.

Once you start focusing on where you can unplug from the outer world and plug in to your family, you will find pockets of time that have been overlooked by current habits and routines.

The second part of the equation is to teach your family the lesson that how you speak not only to each other, but about each other, is a family treasure and one to be protected. Yes, all families irritate each other at times and need to vent. When doing so though, remember how you have felt when you have heard that someone you care about has said something negative or unflattering about you to others. What is said may be simply a moment of frustration or even trying to be cool, but the other person you are venting to remembers it and many times, repeats it and it lives on. Keep that thought close when you choose your words. It breaks my heart when I see children standing with their parent in a line at the grocery store in the summer and I hear the parent telling the cashier that they cannot wait for school to start so they can get rid of these kids and send them back to school so that they are out of their hair. I see the strained smile on the child and the pain in their eyes. It makes me wonder if the parent would think it was as funny if their spouse or significant other told strangers and friends on a regular basis that they cannot wait for them to be out of their sight. How we speak about our loved ones is teaching them how to speak about us, our family, and their future loved ones as they grow and have their own families. Words linger and energy begets energy. The more positive we speak, the more positive we receive.

Strong, healthy, happy, trusted, valued family relationships will strengthen every aspect of your life and reduce your stress. There will be growing pains as you implement changes, but just like when you weaned your baby, potty-trained your toddler, or started a new exercise routine, the effort will be so worth it. Your little ones will grow into loving adults that seek out time to share their lives with you. There is no greater gift.

Loretta Mohl

Self-Limiting Belief Buster Loretta Mohl is the creator of the Focused Intention Technique that has guided hundreds of career women, since 1998, to live lives they love through the power of listening, reflecting, and gaining clarity around the intentions that matter most for each. She is the author of *Bust Your Stress: Heal Your Past* and *Get a Move on Life, Bust Your Stress: Heal Your Past to Get Your Happiness On, and Unlimited You.* For additional tips and strategies on busting loose of hidden beliefs, join my Facebook page https://www.facebook.com/ResetMindsetExpert, or to learn more about how your limiting beliefs define you, take my limiting belief assessment by going to my website:

🏠 www.lorettamohl.com.

✉️ lorettamohl@gmail.com

🏠 www.focusedinentiontechnique.com

f www.facebook.com/focusedintentiontechniqueprocess

f www.facebook.com/ResetMindsetExpert

in www.linkedin.com/in/lorettamohl

Ⓢ Skype: lorettam11

📞 (1) 305 848 2441 or (52) 984 130 2681

Location: Playa del Carmen, Mexico

LESSON 17

Transforming Limiting Beliefs for Smart Parenting

By Loretta Mohl

~~~

</div>

"We learn our belief systems as very little children, and then we move through life creating experiences to match our beliefs. Look back in your own life and notice how often you have gone through the same experience."

– Louise L. Hay

I have a strong conviction that all people deserve to live a life without limiting beliefs. Everyone is entitled to live a healthy, robust life filled with promise, love, and happiness.

Being a mom to my beautiful son has been the greatest challenge of my life, as well as my greatest joy. His arrival opened the door to the many wonderful changes throughout my life. He was a gift from the universe. I call him my "Miracle Baby" and often tell him how grateful I am that he chose me to be his parent.

Today, I live my life with passion, purpose, and I see endless possibilities, but that hasn't always been my truth. I was raised in an environment fraught with instability and danger. Learning to survive each day was my main priority. A positive mindset, self-esteem, confidence, and responsible role models were lacking in my life.

My decision to heal myself and help others has shaped who I am today. My personal journey started during a time when energetic modalities were not widely accepted. I began my career by studying to be a psychiatric nurse. I was determined to understand the cycle of addiction. The next step was Neuro-Linguistic Programming (NLP). From there I moved to Reiki, Quantum Touch, Peruvian Shamanism, and Theta Healing.

My path wasn't easy. I lacked a clear roadmap and was presented with many doubts and questions along the way. Why was life so damn hard? Why were so many people suffering? Why were so many willing to accept unhappy lives devoid of passion? Why did bad things happen, especially to good people? During my healing journey, I eventually found the answers to all these questions, and so much more.

I was determined to find the root cause of the limitations and emotional pain that was locked deep within me. After years of intense study, research, and practical observation, I discovered that the answers to most of our problems reside within the wisdom of our bodies. In 2009, I created a system known as FIT (Focused Intention Technique) that teaches people how to identify, root out, and eliminate limiting beliefs. Since those times, I have helped thousands experience the freedom, joy, success, and healthy relationships that they so longed for.

The way we view ourselves and the world around us is shaped by our childhood experiences. This is particularly true when it comes to our beliefs regarding our potential for success, happiness, and feelings of self-worth.

Even in the most stable families, as a child matures, goes to school, and interacts with peers, the carefree passion that was once natural and easy becomes subdued and tempered by the expectations of others. Subtle shaming and criticism create feelings of doubt and insecurity. As a child moves into adolescence, he may begin to believe the negative impressions that have been implanted into his subconscious mind.

Over time, limiting beliefs become deeply ingrained in the brain's circuitry. During our adult lives, more layers of stresses and disappointments are added, which reinforce these limiting beliefs.

The following real-life event is an example of how the beliefs of parents can adversely affect the wellbeing of their children and how people can change for the better when conditions change. This is a story of a mother who took in a teenage girl who was being adversely impacted by a family break-up.

"A young female high school student who came from a dysfunctional family asked me for help. Her grades were dropping and she was feeling overwhelmed and stressed due to family problems. Her parents had a history of marital problems relating to their upbringings and personal life choices. Their constant drama relating to their own deep issues prevented them from expressing the love that this girl needed, and as a result, her life was in turmoil.

They had very high expectations of her but were unable to provide emotional support that she required. When her parents separated, her mom moved to another city, and she stayed with her dad. He was often away, so she was left to do as she pleased. She began to look for affection in all the wrong places, which further diminished her self-esteem. She was expected to support herself, but no guidance or instructions were provided on how to do it.

When she moved in with us, we set out two conditions. 1) Chores and schoolwork had to completed on a daily basis, and 2) She had to keep us informed of her whereabouts. She had a low opinion of herself and lacked confidence. Whenever we praised her by pointing out how capable and talented she was, it would bring her to tears, and she would say, "But I'm not capable, I am going to let everyone down, I'm a huge disappointment." When we discussed her future plans for college, she said, "What's the point? I'm not good enough to get in." Her marks were low when she came to live with us. Initially, she had a self-esteem boost and some scholastic successes. However, in a short period she began to self-sabotage, testing us in various manners to see if we really cared for her. She didn't believe that she was worthy of our praise, support, and love.

After only two phone sessions with Loretta Mohl, we noticed a remarkable turn-around and improvement in her overall demeanor and emotional state. She immersed herself back into her schoolwork, and within two weeks, she increased her grade average by 15 percent. She became hopeful, optimistic, and with a spark in her eyes, she began to plan her future. I am amazed at how much she has changed in such a short time. Thanks to Loretta's FIT system, this young girl has eliminated many of her limiting beliefs. She is now able to experience the freedom, joy, success, and healthy relationships that she so longed for."

My mission is to provide moms with simple, easy to understand strategies that can be integrated into their daily lives so they can empower their children, as well as themselves. All children deserve positive reinforcement from their parents. This support allows them to move beyond limiting beliefs and blossom into healthy, loving adults.

Here are eight practical tips to help Moms embrace their value, bring harmony to chaos, and live with passion and purpose.

1. **Name and claim self-limiting beliefs.** The top three issues that paralyze people are: Self Worth (*I'm not good enough*), Doubt (*I'm not capable* or *there's not enough time*), and Fear of Change *(It's really tough out there*, or *I'm not smart enough to make this work)*. You must identify it before you can change it.

2. **Apply the Focused Intention Technique** to eliminate limiting beliefs standing in the way of happiness and balance. The key is to apply a fail-proof, step-by-step process that fixes the fatal flaws that block joy and prosperity.

3. **Start each day with focus and intention** regarding the most important thing that you need to change. More than 80 percent of our thinking is unconscious. Clarity brings conscious and unconscious beliefs into alignment.

4. **Connect to and listen to your body every day.** Awareness helps to bring limitations to the surface where they can be released. Place your right hand over your heart, feel the pace of your breathing, and be aware of where you are holding tension.

5. **Connect to your soul.** Tune in to your joyous creative center. It's time to leap out of your head and dive into your heart, wherein lies the source of loving acts, random kindness, and generosity.

6. **Stay open.** Stay open. It's OK to voice big dreams and express your deepest desires. Honor and nurture them with optimism, reverence, and respect.

7. **Get to the root cause of limiting beliefs, explore the deeper feelings attached to each one, and release them.** It takes courage to see and speak your own truth and become empowered. Freedom awaits you.

8. **Ask for and take action with support.** Find a coach or mentor that you trust to help you release the self-limiting beliefs that are

standing in your way. For those who need one-on-one support, do your due diligence to find the right fit. Oprah Winfrey has often said, "You get in life what you have the courage to ask for." I believe that knowing what you want and sharing that desire with a trusted guide is always a great place to begin.

Take action. Even the smallest step will help move you forward. Your first steps don't have to be perfect, just headed in the right direction. And be sure to acknowledge yourself when you've taken that step.

Nora Cabrera and Nachhi Randhawa

Nora Cabrera and Nachhi Randhawa specialize in expertly guiding heart-centered entrepreneurs, professionals, and creatives who are ready to step out of old patterns that are not working anymore, heal their money stories, and move into the world to share their unique gifts joyfully.

Their signature "Alchemy of Success Private Coaching" and "Vision Board Quest™ Certified Coach Training" programs are making a profound difference in the lives of coaches, healers, and entrepreneurs everywhere. Their unique approach in healing from within, mastering money, powerful marketing strategies, personal growth, and breakthrough coaching cultivate a holistic approach to living and thriving in the world.

🏠 **www.3BlessingsSuccess.com**

🐦 **www.twitter.com/3BlessingsInst**

f **www.facebook.com/3BlessingsSuccess**

How to Get Your Dreams Back in a Life Filled with Your Family's Needs, Wants, and Dreams

By Nora Cabrera & Nachhi Randhawa

~~~

Motherhood is not easy, we're sure you'll agree. And it's never quite what you expected it to be in your mind when you were planning it, is it? But once you're a mother, you experience a love like no other and a determination to create the best possible life for your child or children, no matter the circumstances.

What seems to happen then is the dreams that you held, before you were a mother, seem to fall by the wayside. Life becomes so busy with the long list of to-do's and ensuring the needs and wants of your family that the dreams that once took center stage in your heart and mind for yourself retreat to the back and become just mere whispers. Or we abandon them all together—believing that it would be impossible to serve and care for our families, as well as pursue our own dreams—or even worse, we convince ourselves that they just don't matter anymore.

We are both mothers. Between us, we have three sons and a daughter. And we are deeply committed to being loving, supportive, present mothers in each of our families. And we are also in the business of helping women re-discover their truth, heal their money stories, and uncover the whispers of their hearts and souls. We have both had profound experiences with "Visioning" work in many different forms throughout the years. So we would like to take a moment to briefly share one of our many "Visioning" stories:

NACHHI'S STORY:

In 2006, after relocating to be closer to our family, we were in search of the perfect house to raise our family. For a good year, it seemed that we were looking at house after house, and our attempts of finding that perfect place to call home were becoming futile. In mid-2007, I started working with visioning and seeing how I wanted my life to unfold and what I wanted to experience, both personally and with my family. With this amazing visioning work, I suddenly had an "aha" moment as we were standing inside a model home one day, and immediately pulled out my camera and took a few photos of us in elegant settings.

I quickly went home and wrote a description of exactly what my husband and I both wanted in a dream home and then I pasted that description, along with the photos of us, right on my first vision board. Two days later, we found ourselves inside what would become our "home." As I sat on the concrete-stamped patio bench in the spa-like garden, I knew I was home.

The next day, we drew up papers for the house with our realtor and went out to celebrate our new house over dinner that evening. Of course, the Universe wanted to be sure that's exactly what we wanted, so while there was a test or two along the way, that experience certainly taught me the power of fully believing in our visions while surrendering at the same time. After countering back twice, our realtor gave us a bit of a scare with what looked like a price-bidding war that was about to happen. And yet, I had this complete faith that that house was ours, so after taking a few minutes to think, we told her we'd given her our final offer, and we trusted that the house would be ours.

That night as we were talking about the house as if it were already ours, our six-year-old daughter asked to light a candle and make a wish for the house to be ours. Together, we lit the candle and made our wish. The very next day, the realtor called and congratulated us on our new home. And at the official signing, she asked exactly what happy dance I was doing to create for such a smooth sale. All I could do was smile and say a silent thank you to the Universe!

WHY VISIONING WORK IS POWERFUL AND ESSENTIAL:

We've all heard that vision boards can be powerful. And if you've created one before and have had items from your board manifest, you know that you're not really sure why it worked. And maybe you've heard of vision boards before but haven't tried it or got stuck after the customary images: house, car, vacation pic, and how much money you'd like to bring in to your experience. We've been there for all of those!

We've come to believe that when created within a clear space of purpose, intention, and from the depths of our hearts (and out of our heads), vision boards are powerful tools for our spirits and our subconscious minds. They are like the GPS system connecting Spirit with our physical realities and subconscious minds. And for those of you who don't know, our subconscious mind is usually in charge—not our conscious mind. We're talking 70%-90% in charge, in the driver's seat of all our motivations, actions, and ahem, habits.

Take a moment to close your eyes and think of one of the happiest moments in your life. Now take another moment to bring to mind something you deeply desire and what would it be like if you already had that. Great. Now we'd like to ask you—how were you able to "see" both those situations? Did you read words in your mind's eye? Smell something particular or hear something? Chances are the biggest sense you used for both experiences was visual: you experienced both in images. Can you see why images then could be so powerful in your vision board work and intentions?

We would like to guide you through a simple process to get started. There are many ways we take this powerful work very deep with our clients and we would like to offer you three simple steps right now to begin your Vision Board Quest™:

Step 1: Get clear on your desires. Getting really clear on exactly what you'd like to experience or manifest into your physical reality is key in aligning powerfully with your visions. Because when we are aligned from a connected and authentic heart space, manifesting literally becomes effortless as we start to live and breathe the visions within, which then makes way for them to be made manifest. To do this and tap into your deepest inner desires, carve out some sacred time, light a candle, use some essential oils, and start brainstorming on paper exactly what you'd like to experience or create in your life. Put on a timer for five minutes and really get deep into getting your visions on paper. After you complete this process, go back through each vision you've listed and feel into the vision as if it were here right now. Does it light you up? Does it give you exactly the experience you yearn for? Circle all those visions that are deeply calling to you.

Step 2: Get your board, glue, scissors, and all your favorite magazines. Search for all those pictures that represent the visions you just wrote down. If you don't find an exact image for any of your visions, do a google search and print the perfect image representing the exact vision in your mind's eye. Now it's time to start gluing. First, add a photo of yourself in your happiest and most joyful state, right in the middle of that vision board. Around that photo, write five to six words that express who you are as a person and the life you're creating for yourself. Now place images representing your visions onto the vision board. Enjoy this process! Be creative, express, use glitter, stickers, and make it an authentic representation of yourself. *NOTE: As a mom, feel free to make a vision boarding date with your child or children and get them involved. This is a wonderful process to share with your school-age children and teach them early on that they can truly create their life by design.

Step 3: Place your vision board in a place you will see it every day, where you will feel called to spend time visiting, meditating, and visualizing upon the images on your board. Look at your vision board, close your eyes, and enter that heart space where the visions are fully made manifest and you are fully experiencing them. Really see them, feel them, breathe your visions. And then enjoy your day, your life, fully knowing and trusting in the Universal powers. Trust the journey and celebrate what you have created on your board, knowing that what is for your highest good is already on its way to you. And so it is.

This is a simple way to begin your visioning work, which is really, at a deeper level, your soul's work. Trust the visions in your heart and begin your journey today.

We wish you infinite love, light, and blessings.

Danielle Marggraf

Danielle Marggraf is a writer, speaker, Energy, Money, and Mindset Coach, and single mom of two. She is a guest speaker and lecturer for Institute for Integrative Nutrition and has been published in numerous health and wellness publications, both in print and online. Danielle supports women, entrepreneurs, healers, and holistic practitioners to activate their innate ability to manifest, to empower and inspire them to create, heal, clear, and release blocks to attract more money into their lives so they can focus on what's really important—fun, freedom, and family!

✉ danielle@innermoneygoddess.com

f www.facebook/daniellemarggraf.com

⌂ www.innermoneygoddess.com

LESSON 19

$\mathcal{ACTIVATE}$ Your Inner Money Goddess: Create Your Ultimate Life!

By Danielle Marggraf

~~~

We are born to create as humans, and as mothers, we are the ultimate creators. I have been reborn twice. Once when my daughter was born and then when my son was born twenty-one months later. My life was never the same, and although I had prepared for the sleepless nights and the crying, my life changed in ways that I had never really anticipated. As my family expanded and grew, as I expanded and grew, our family unit divided. This is a lesson in re-activating the power within you and creating your ultimate life. You will leave this feeling empowered, inspired, creative, and excited about the possibilities for you and your family.

When my children were three months and twenty months, I knew my marriage was over. We lived in a small two-bedroom apartment, and as the stress and tension of our living situation escalated, my body deteriorated as I held onto the stress. I was getting sick. Fast forward ten months later, I moved in with my parents eight hundred miles away from my home with nothing but my children. I had no money and no direction. It was all surreal. I had these beliefs like, "I'm not the type that gets divorced." "My family was just beginning." "I have two babies and the best times of our lives were ahead of us."

I was also depressed and anxious and had no idea how I was going to get through this. I knew I couldn't stay, as the relationship was over long before I even realized it. I had compromised myself to stay for as long as I did, and I lost myself—maybe I never really knew who I was. I was depleted and empty and worked on autopilot, taking care of my babies and trying to figure out a way to get out of this mess. I felt hopeless, powerless, stuck, and deeply sad. I felt as though I hit bottom. I cried all the time, was scared, and yet I could not collapse, I couldn't fall apart, because I was responsible for two babies that needed me in every way possible.

After I landed at my parents house, I spent months just waking up and going through the motions of living. I was in survival. I was at the base existence of humanity. I did nothing other than feed, clothe, and change my kids; I cried a lot and wore sunglasses to try to hide my pain from my babies. I went outside as much as I could to play with them and stroll with them. I held them close and they kept me alive. They kept me from hiding under the covers and dissolving into the mattress and blankets and disappearing into a vast, deep, and long sleep.

Every morning and every night before I went to bed, I would write, pouring out all of my emotions, writing about my day, how I spent it, my fears, my deep insecurities, feeling rejected, abandoned, alone, like a failure.

I spent months in this state of anguish and all while not bringing in a penny. This was not the plan—the plan was for me to be a stay-at-home mom. I knew my heart wasn't into going back to my old profession. I started to do a lot of research. I already had my yoga certification and I was attuned to Reiki Master level. I was and still am a self-help junkie, and I loved health and wellness. I found Institute for Integrative Nutrition, and it resonated immediately and that scared me. I didn't trust myself, and yet, there was still this small voice inside of me that tugged and nudged.

I followed this nudge.

I didn't know how I would get the money, and I prayed and hoped and I released and I manifested the exact amount of money for the tuition that week. I signed up, and although I was scared, I was certain I had finally uncovered the most important thing that we need to make change, to move forward, to heal. HOPE.

This one decision spiraled me into a positive energy vortex that kept opening doors, people, and opportunities that to this day has not stopped.

So what did I learn that is valuable that I want to share with you and that I share with each of my clients? YOU HAVE THE POWER WITHIN YOU. It is within us all the time. YOU are the creator. It is within your power to use the universal laws and create the life that you desire. On the outside, don't be surprised if naysayers—"realists "—don't believe you, or judge or even criticize. It is their own ignorance that keeps them stuck and small. I ask that you suspend your belief of what you think you know and allow me to guide you in this new way of creating wealth consciousness so you can revolutionize your life and that of your family.

I have gone from zero to over six figures in four months. I manifested a three-bedroom house, a new car, money, a love relationship, new likeminded friends, travel, a supportive mentor, and I keep creating. It is the human experience to want more, to never be finished desiring. Give yourself permission to desire and know that you are worthy, deserving, and enough to receive. Be in gratitude for your now as you allow waves of desire to float into the Universe, knowing you will attract that which is a match for you.

Stress is a big creative killer. I challenge you to manage your stress and not allow your stress to control you. Stress comes in many forms. So many moms get into this Superhuman zone where they feel if they can't or choose to not do it all—work, kids, business, relationship, exercise, cook, clean, meditate, friends etc.--that they somehow are not living up to some set standard. I have doubted my abilities. I have judged my ability to be present and happy and joyful, all why juggling that of two parents. I balance so many balls in the air, and I know when I have reached my limit. The first step for moms to manifest is to start with self-care. Love yourself and your family enough to take care of yourself—mind, body, and spirit. Raise your vibration by nurturing yourself and treating yourself as a worthy part of your family. Let me tell you right from the jumpstart that this will not look like it did before you had children. I think there is this perceived notion to go to an hour and a half yoga class or meditate for forty-five minutes or go to the spa, and what I have learned is that it all looks different. For instance, I loved working out and would spend an hour at the gym daily. Now my workouts look a little more sporadic. When my little ones were babies, and I was adjusting to life alone with them, I might have been able to fit in ten minutes of exercise at a time. At first, I didn't think it was making a difference, and then I went a spell without any exercise and realized those ten-minute sessions really added up. Yoga may not be the Om Zen you're used to. It may be a few poses to stretch and breath and ground in between breakfast and lunch, or while one naps and the other watches a show. These simple and short self-care routines will support you to be more grounded, more relaxed, and help release stress. Spa days may be the thing of the past for you temporarily, and all that means is to improvise with a lavender-salt-infused warm bath, where you can close your eyes for ten minutes and meditate or visualize your desires.

So now let the FUN begin! Let's start Manifesting!

Follow these Manifesting Tips:

1. Decide what it is you want to manifest.

2. Have a visual anchor that symbolizes that which you are intending to experience (in a picture or object).

3. Imagine with all of your senses your desired outcome being real.

4. Be aware of guidance that will lead you to your manifestation.

Stay aware of these points while you are manifesting:

1. Don't try to make things happen. Trying too hard is actually fear. That will block what it is you desiring.

2. Don't ask repeatedly from a place of worry or fear after you ask for what you desire. When you repeatedly hold a vision coming from a place of worry, you are telling the Universe that you don't believe you will really get it. Feel a sense of peace after you have asked, and then expect that you will receive it.

3. Release! Let go after you have made your request. Trust that you can release your intention and it will be honored.

4. Be aware of guidance that follows the manifestation process. If you're stuck, ask a question about what you need to do next. It may be a thought or a feeling.

Be aware of patterns, because guidance comes in patterns.

It is absolutely possible for you to have the life that you desire. If it's in your mind, it can manifest into matter.

Jamie Anne Love

Jamie is a multifaceted entrepreneur and public speaker with businesses in import/exports, health and wellness, and self-development. She has a Mortuary Science Degree from MATC, and is a Certified Facilitator with Access Consciousness, Certified Colon Hydro therapist, and Owner of South Shore Cleansing Spa. She uses tools that give others the ability to be present in their life in every moment, without judgment of them or anyone else. Jamie's unique creative approach encourages you to let go of what isn't working for you in favor of pragmatic tools that can easily transform emotional confusion with any relationship into insightful clarity with the ease.

✉ accessjamieanne@gmail.com

⌂ www.jamieannelove.com

⌂ www.ancientworldtrade.com

Meditation in the Moment

By Jamie Anne Love

～～～

What if we can learn from our children? To see these amazing little beings with wonder and sparkle in their eyes, with no worry, no fear, and complete trust is miraculous. Coming from a place of innocence, they are ready to explore this magical world with the willingness to be mesmerized by what we see as ordinary. What if that is why we are here? What if we are here on this planet to delight in our life, like our children? What if we woke up every day looking for our next adventure? Is it possible to let go of what holds us back from living in that space?

When I was pregnant, I would hear women talking about how their lives were never the same after they had children. How all their priorities changed and what was important before wasn't so significant. It caused me to wonder if I would be a good mom, and what is a good mom anyway? I remember my childhood and how amazing my mother was with me. How could I measure up? What if you being you is exactly what your children require? Who knew being a Mom would be the most rewarding job I have ever had?

One of my favorite Mommy moments occurred when my youngest daughter, Lydia, was three years old. It was one of those typical days of doing laundry, searching through my cookbooks for yet another way to cook chicken, and watching Lydia play in the backyard. As I looked up for a brief moment, I saw my daughter running toward me, calling out, "Mommy, Mommy, look at the beautiful flower I found!" To be honest, most of the time, I did not take those few moments to really look at what she was bringing me. She was constantly finding small treasures to show me and I was always too busy, trying to get as much done in a day as I possibly could. As if I was going to get some trophy for having the cleanest house on the block. For some reason, I did not do that this time. As she came close, she opened her little hand to show me the teeniest tiny flower, and said "I picked the prettiest one for you, Mommy." She pointed out the tiny petals, the yellow color in the center, and the miniscule teeny green leaves under the petals. In that moment, I realized all those times she was trying to get my attention were actually times that I took for granted and could have been moments where we could have connected on a deeper level.

Today, Lydia has no recollection of this priceless moment. But it has always stayed with me, ranking as one of my most life-changing experiences. At that moment, my heart was filled with gratitude for Lydia and her special talent for seeing the smallest details, and for her awareness of such beauty. Viewing that lovely flower that morning was a unique meditation for me. It was a beginning to an awareness that my life is a meditation. Sometimes the most beautiful moments in our lives are the ones that we don't plan, we just experience. To this day, every time I pick a flower, I recall the memory in the backyard with Lydia, and smile. It will forever be a part of me.

Mothers really have a very special opportunity that many do not... to see life through the eyes of their children. When you find yourself stopped in your tracks by the smallest of moments, you know just how blessed you are.

There are so many moments in each day that are unique little meditations, if we allow them to be. A moment of gratitude and vulnerability. One of *pause.* Moments that can trigger you to contemplate life in a whole new way. Or shift your entire perspective on how you view yourself and the world. It's the little moments that take your breath away that are the ones you will remember for a lifetime. We mothers are blessed to have these little teachers, with so much to give, showing up in these tiny bodies.

To help me remember to embrace those beautiful unplanned moments, I post little reminder notes and stick them on my mirror in the bathroom or on the refrigerator. Notes like…**"How can today be better than I could possibly imagine?"**

"What would it take for me to be aware of the magical moments in my day?"

"How can I create more ease, joy, and abundance in my life right away?"

I read the questions out loud and allow them to magnify my awareness. I don't use my mind to figure them out. I open up the space to let God show me how amazing my life is at this very moment. Today. Right now. Isn't that the purpose of meditation? Not to allow our thoughts, feelings, or emotions from the past, and worries of the future, to cloud our mind. Learning techniques to disconnect from anxiety, anger, or frustration can help to create a space of empowerment and inner peace, even in the mist of chaos. Inner peace creates a space so we can expand our awareness, unlocking us from what holds us back to live in the present moment. To truly live in *bliss*, NOW.

ADDING LOVE EXERCISE: (1-5 MINUTES)

Use this meditation whenever you need more space. You will be amazed at the difference it makes for you and how you relate to your family.

Close your eyes, imagine you are expanding your heart, filling your home with love. Pause for a few seconds, or up to a minute.

Now, let your love expand through your whole town or city. Pause again.

Now, let your love expand across your whole state. Pause again.

Expand your love across the country. Again pause.

Then expand your love across the continent. Pause.

Extend your love around this beautiful planet. Pause.

Now let your love extend into space and throughout the galaxy, touching all the stars and all the other planets and beyond. Pause.

Now what space are you in?

Doing this exercise, you become more *centered*, allowing the space you need to *BREATHE*. Your breath is so important with any meditation you do. Just paying attention to your breath can be a mediation in and of itself.

BREATHING EXERCISE:

Breathing is the key to living. You can live without food for several weeks, you can live without water for a couple of days, but you cannot live without breathing for more than a minute. Bringing attention to your breath is a way to come back to the present moment.

Start with taking a breath in for six seconds and then breathing out for six seconds.

Then work your way up to ten seconds in and out, thirty seconds in and out, or even longer. Breathing in and out equally is the key.

It really can be that easy. You can meditate anywhere, anytime. When you are driving to drop off your children to school, waiting in line at the grocery store, holding and rocking your baby to sleep, while making a meal, and yes, even while you are in the bathroom. Sometimes that's the only place you have a moment to yourself.

Taking time to replenish yourself is key to being a "Happy Mommy." We mothers have a lot more influence than we may even be conscious of to enhance harmony and well-being in our home. You know the saying…"If Momma isn't happy, nobody's happy."

How can we give our best when our cup is only half full, or we feel like we have nothing left to give? How is that being a contribution to our family?

Use these simple meditation techniques to refill your cup. I have found that when I give to myself first, everyone around me benefits. Remember that when you board an airplane, they give instructions, in an event of an emergency, to put on your own oxygen mask first before placing one on your child. How can you help you or your child if you're passed out in the seat next them? How can you be an asset to yourself and your family if you have completely depleted your energy?

Drawing yourself a nice long bath, lighting a scented candle, getting a massage, or going to get a pedicure can be ways of taking care of you. Allowing time for yourself is not being selfish. It is a necessity. To have the very best *you* show up for your family, you must be balanced, de-stressed, happy, and feeling vital.

Yes, we are here to teach our children. And if we give ourselves permission to stay present, stay in the here and now, the real magic happens…our children teach us, too.

Wendy Silvers

Wendy Silvers is the founder of the Million Mamas Movement, an organization dedicated to women and children thriving globally. She is also a Spiritual Midwife, helping women birth and earth their visions into being; an Agape Licensed Spiritual Therapist; an Inspirational Speaker; and director of the Agape Parenting Ministry. Wendy teaches Compassionate Parenting and Communication. She is a published author and a contributor to the Huffington Post. For decades, Wendy has immersed herself in the studies of psychology, transformation, parenting, and personal growth. In an earlier career, Wendy was a celebrity, music, and film publicist in the entertainment industry.

- ✉ wendy@wendysilvers.com
- ✉ wendy@millionmamasmovement.org
- ⌂ www.wendysilvers.com
- ⌂ www.millionmamasmovement.org
- 🎤 blogtalkradio.com/wendysilvers
- ⌂ huffingtonpost.com/wendy-silvers
- f www.facebook.com/mamawendysilvers
- f www.facebook.com/millionmamasmovement
- 🐦 www.twitter.com/wendysilvers

- www.twitter.com/millionmamas
- Skype: wendymillionmamasmovement
- www.instagram.com/wendy_silvers
- www.youtube.com/user/MillionMamasMovement
- plus.google.com/+MaMaWendy

LESSON 21

Rock Yo' Mama Self — 4 Pathways to Activate your W-O-M-B Wisdom

By Wendy Silvers

~~~~

There's a power within you that is unstoppable, a creative impulse that wants to express itself, a wisdom that is empowered by a love that knows no bounds. We all have it, for we all have access to this Great Mother energy. It is native to women, for we have the ability to create and destroy, literally. I call this womb wisdom. The invitation is always there, it's whether we RSVP. Mother love is a force of nature. Sacred. Intense. Fierce. Gentle. Unceasing. Immeasurable. There is no greater power than this Love. It transforms and softens the hardened places within us. This Universal Divine Mother energy sources all people, everywhere.

Mothering, parenting, is the Heart-est work there is. Mothers, and fathers who mother, are the spiritual heart of the family. We are our children's first teachers, their first loves, and their God/Goddesses. To stay sane and serene as we grow our children, we must learn to put the oxygen mask on our face first. We must have boundaries, not walls. We cannot teach what we cannot be. Peace and love are verbs, not nouns.

Nothing, absolutely nothing, comes close to the daily experience I cherish and treasure beyond words—MAMA. The birth of my daughter began the deepest and most fulfilling love affair I've ever experienced. From the second I discovered that I was pregnant, jumping for joy in the bathroom as I looked at the pink line on the pregnancy test stick, there was an alchemical quickening within me. I had this sense that nothing in my world would ever be the same again. And it wasn't. In that singular moment, my relationship to life and the world around me changed. I chose to birth at home, in the bedroom of our tiny apartment, breastfed my daughter until she was three, and implemented the family bed. I felt compelled to provide this baby growing within me with a sacred and gentle entry into this world and to create a home environment that would support our baby's highest and greatest unfoldment. I would not have done anything differently. Well, I would have learned hypno-birthing, or tried orgasmic birth, but that's about it.

From the minute our daughter emerged, I was a different woman. What occurred with my daughter's birth was that an aspect of myself was birthed that would not be denied in speech or action. I was a mother. There was something primal and ancient that got activated within me after giving birth—womb wisdom. I wanted my daughter to have everything that I didn't. I wanted her to know within her bones that she was worthy and loved just for being. To know that she was perfect. No matter what. I wanted her to have her voice and the courage to use it. That meant I had to have mine. Thus my journey began in activating my womb wisdom that continues today.

New Motherhood brought new pressures and responsibilities. I thought that I would work part-time while caring for our child. I was clear that I could not and would not return to my old workplace, which would have required my leaving this precious baby in daycare for nine hours a day. While this choice was a compelling one for me, it created financial hardship for our family and conflict with my husband. I had married a wonderful, talented man whose work experience had been in the theater, not in the boardroom. Yet, he stepped up to this challenge. I had a vision—I was matriculating through classes at the Agape International Spiritual Center to become an Agape Licensed Spiritual Therapist. I was already a hypnotherapist and spiritual medium. I had flirted with the idea that I would become a midwife and help women birth babies the way my midwives had helped me, but after the first week of radical sleep deprivation, I amended that intention. I chose to be a spiritual midwife and to assist women in birthing and earthing the highest and greatest visions for their life. That felt more congruent to me. It also became apparent that I enjoyed helping other mamas parent in a more natural and compassionate way that honored their needs, their family's values, and the needs of their children. My personal passion turned into my teaching compassionate, heart-centered parenting in workshops, and midwifing women's dreams and visions in my private practice.

There's an old saying, "We teach most what we need to learn." This rang true for me in terms of rockin' ma mama self. I teach that, "Getting into a relationship, and, especially, becoming a parent, is like putting Miracle Grow on all the unhealed places within us that are seeking healing." Relationships offer us the greatest portals of transformation and a relationship is only as healthy as the two people in it. It's so easy to point the finger at another, yet when we do this, there are three pointing back at us. It also takes enormous courage to do things differently.

The content of our life is our personal curriculum. We learn how to relate to others from what we see modeled in our families of origin—each family has a different line-up. Typically, there's a smorgasbord of love, fear, shame, judgment with varying mixed messages about money, sex, competition, and loyalty. The message that most of us receive is that there's something wrong with us. For decades, my curriculum was learning to love myself because all I saw was what I thought was wrong with me. As I grew spiritually, this began to shift. I felt deep compassion for the younger me. When I became a mother, I knew that I was entering unchartered territory, yet I had a sense of confidence that hadn't existed before. My challenges had become my greatest learnings.

A huge portal of learning humility and compassion occurred when I experienced a life-altering illness that would render me unpredictably incapacitated for seven years. It was concurrent with my having secondary infertility and moving my mom to an assisted living facility in the town where I lived, as she had dementia. What felt like losing control led me to examine what I really believed spiritually, and to surrender to living in the moment. I began to let go of seeing myself as not good enough, and compassion and empathy became my running buddies. I knew intuitively that in order for me to energize my womb wisdom, I had to completely let go of old, limiting beliefs and choose to actively love and value myself and embrace my self-worth.

The journey to embody our power as mamas may appear to be filled with brambles, burrs, and tears, yet it is truly the path to self-love, self-appreciation, freedom, joy, and harmony in relationships. We can see that our standing in our womb wisdom is what transforms our families and our children's future. Be not afraid—this wisdom is already within you. It's only a matter of giving yourself the opportunity to reveal your innate power.

Here are four pathways that will assist you in activating your W-O-M-B wisdom:

W – Within. Go within to that place and space where time collapses. Take five minutes or fifteen to be in the stillness daily. Access that unstoppable power within that says, *I'm here. I have a right to be here. I matter, and I've got things to say!*

O – Oxygen mask. Fill your well before giving to others. Pause. Turn within. Move your body. Breathe—remember that you cannot breathe in the past nor in the future. When you breathe, you are fully in the present moment.

M – Meditate. Start a Moms Meditation circle. Try different forms of meditation—sitting, walking—and see what fits for you. Meditate while you nurse or feed your baby. Consistent practice will give you an overall sense of wellbeing, calm, and a decrease in stress.

B – Boundaries. Boundaries provide balance between our giving and over-giving. It's so important to know what works and doesn't work for you, and have the language to communicate this. Define what is acceptable and unacceptable for you. You will learn not to over-apologize, justify, or defend. Practice setting boundaries with a sacred buddy and counselor. It may feel unnatural at first, but keep going.

Attunement:

In the fullness of this moment, how very grateful and thankful I am for Love, this love that knows no bounds, that is formless, shapeless, yet always present. How grateful I am for the unceasing Divine mother love that flows to, through, and as my very life. It is my source and the source and supply of every man, woman, and child that comes to the planet. I speak the word for courage and strength within each mother to rock her mama self. I call forth the activation of the womb wisdom within them. I know that there is no limit to their good. All that they need is within them. Right where they are, love is, peace is, good is. Now and forever more.

And so it is.

Sherry Rothwell

Sherry Rothwell is a business "strategista" who helps spiritually-based entrepreneurs create sumptuous programs and packages that spark the soul and sell. Sherry models a multi-passionate approach in her work by combining both her nutrition savvy, to boost your power to attract, and her writing talents, to help you weave words that wow! Sherry's unique approach to business helps you stay in feminine flow, by working in tune with the moon and through "slow marketing," a sensual and sustainable path for making a living doing what you love!

You can connect her at www.SherryRothwell.com or on Facebook:

www.facebook.com/moonmaven

LESSON 22

"Seasonality" — A time for everything, and everything in its time

By Sherry Rothwell

~~~

Ironically, becoming a mother simultaneously kick-starts our drive into high gear, and at the same time, "puts the foot on the brake," with round-the-clock responsibility.

It seems to be a universal phenomenon that women give birth to their most powerful creative urges, while simultaneously giving birth to themselves as mothers (many women attest that this heightened creativity begins early on in pregnancy).

Could it be part of the divine plan that, with the birth of a child, we are also wired to give birth to a strong desire to manifest positive changes in the world?

And after all, who better than a mother high on love hormones to recreate the world?!

MY STORY...

Being a driven young mama myself, early motherhood was a conflicting time for me.

I struggled with the story that my passions compromised my mothering—and that my mothering compromised my work. I often felt like I wasn't doing a very good job of anything. In many ways, I felt unable to give myself fully to either—and living only to a fraction of my capacity.

There was still *soooo* much more that I desired to create and do in my life. I thought, "If only I had more time, *then* I could free my family financially *and spend more quality time with my kids."*

I was overcome with futility—and seriously perplexed by my seemingly contradictory urges to fully embody my role as a nurturer—and at the same time, fulfill my dreams, passions, and purpose as a woman.

BUT A STORY IS ALL IT WAS.

It's a worldview that bullies us mamas into believing that we can't have it all (and shouldn't).

It's the voice of the collective feminine "pain body" that says, "Being a good mom requires that we simply put our dreams on the shelf."

These voices convince us that our children's highest needs will be compromised if we fashion our dreams in concert with fulfilling our role as a mother.

Yet spirit does not speak to us through guilt, fear, or doubt.

The voice of spirit, rather, speaks to through inspiration, affirmation, and trust. And through our soul's yearnings—your dreams, ideas, and passions are divinely inspired!

Instead of doubting inspiration, it's time that we start doubting doubt itself.

What we are really called to do as mothers is to embody and model living fully, self-expressed in the truth of who we are, so that our children can naturally and easily do that too.

In fact, the future wellbeing of the next generation rests on us mamas to intuit how to live in consensus with our children, with all of our needs met and fulfilled together.

Starting with trading in the either/or mentality, for a both/and one.

BACK TO THE STORY....

Two years ago, I finally arrived at what I thought would be the mecca of motherhood. After eleven years of being devoted to working at home to be with my kids, they both entered school fulltime. I went from five to ten hours of focused, kid-free work time a week to thirty hours a week, and guess what?

Nothing changed! I still found that I had all the same excuses.

HERE IS THE TRUTH.

Time poverty is our own creation.

I discovered that the only way out of feeling victimized by time is to accept 100 percent full responsibility for how I relate to it.

I had to ask myself questions like: am I investing this time or simply spending it? Am I really present? or Am I simply doing time (literally and figuratively)?

HERE'S HOW I CAME TO REALIZE IT WAS ALL IN MY HEAD...

Very soon after I made the switch from holistic nutrition consulting to business coaching, I had four conversations with women over the age of fifty who were still using their family as the number one excuse for why they couldn't have the life or business they truly desired—even though their children had long since left the nest!

It also occurred to me that I had, on more than one occasion, heard single women without children complain about not having enough time, as well.

Suddenly, it became crystal clear to me that the whole "I can't (fill in the blank) because I am a mom and I don't have time" line was simply a catchall excuse—and one that we are all too quick to validate each other for. I think it is time that we *call out* the "I don't have time...." excuse for what it is—a way to avoid saying "yes" to secret desires that we are afraid to commit to and fulfill—and to avoid saying "no" to stuff that we think we should say "yes" to but don't really want to.

So let me ask you, are you using motherhood, money, or time poverty as an excuse to keep you from creating the life you really want?

And are you sure that the minute your kids are in school (or move out of the house), that things are going to change for you and you'll suddenly be free of all your excuses?

Or do you sense that if you don't change your relationship to time sooner than later, you might find yourself living into the same old story of limitation, lack, and time poverty five, ten, or twenty years from now?

If you are concerned, don't lose heart! If you feel time-starved, overwhelmed, or depleted—and you're ready to shift that—then you are going to love what I am about to share with you about how you can manage your energy, instead of your time.

Getting into "right relationship" with time is not about time management, but rather it is about how we relate to time by shifting our internal "time paradigm" in four ways:

#1 The first step is to decide right now that you will never again let yourself say the words out loud, "I don't have enough time" to avoid deciding and committing to what you *really want*, or when what you really mean to say is "no." From this day forward, let your "yes" mean "yes" and your "no" mean "no." #2 The next step is shifting how you conceptualize time—from linear to cyclic. Linear time feels like it is running out and like everything needs to get done and happen all at once. Cyclic time feels like it is coming back round again.

Nature reveals to us that time moves in cycles.

Fortunately, as women, we cannot separate ourselves from this sacred truth because menstruation affords us a monthly reminder. One of the best-kept feminine secrets to managing our energy is discovering how our energy waxes and wanes throughout the moon's cycle.

By being aware of how our energy cycles, we can plan all of our household, work, and business tasks in tune with the moon—allowing our endeavours to be supported in sync with our internal feminine clock.

Here is a glimpse of how our energy flows with the moon: Waning Moon (energy recedes): Cleanse and Clear New Moon (energy internalized): Vision and Plan Waxing Moon (energy builds): Gestate and Relate Full Moon (energy expands): Create and Celebrate

I liken attuning my own monthly and weekly rhythm to the moon's cycles as being a metaphorical shelf for time. Just as a home without furniture, shelves, closets, or drawers would be hard to keep comfy, tidy, and organized—life without a rhythm feels unsatisfying, unproductive, and ineffectual.

By being aware of how your cycle impacts your energy, you'll find that there is indeed a perfect time for everything—and that everything unfolds in its perfect timing.

#3 It's important to realize that the root of the problem is not that we don't have enough time—*it's that we don't have enough energy.*

The beautiful thing about attuning to our natural rhythm is that it allows us to feel tireless.

And this time, it's the body that demonstrates this truth.

Have you ever noticed that your lungs never tire of breathing? Nor does your heart of beating? That's because rhythms inherently conserve our energy *and naturally pace our lives.*

Syncing with the moon builds our energy. Rhythm maintains it. And the secret to feeling timeless is presence.

#4 Call yourself into the present moment, by plugging the "energy leaks" in your life.

What do you lose energy to? What unattainable ideals, situations, or people drain you? Is your mind tied up with future worries or lost in pain from the past? Do you suppress your health problems, or escape your emotions through food, drugs, or alcohol?

Your energy is your most precious commodity. Give your full attention to shifting how you relate to time—*because what you focus on expands.*

You might just be pleasantly surprised to discover that you've *always* had more than enough time…for what truly matters.

Jenna Tasker

Jenna Tasker, The Rainbow Goddess, is the founder of TheRawCalendar. com, a new online resource guide, as well as Raw Sunshine Retreats, offering planning and development of retreats, classes, workshops, events, and coaching. Experienced and trained within all avenues of the raw food community, she has been honored to work with some of the world's leading Raw Food Pioneers.

Through intensive Life Mastery training, Jenna has come to recognize that her greatest joy comes from supporting others along their transformational journeys by offering inspiration and guidance, as they explore, learn and transition into living the life they love—the life of their dreams!

✉ TheRainbowGoddess@yahoo.com

⌂ www.RawSunshineRetreats.com

⌂ www.therawcalendar.com

⌂ www.wakingupraw.com

f www.facebook.com/RawSunshineRetreats

LESSON 23

Waking Up Raw

By Jenna Tasker

~~~~~

HEALTHY, ORGANIC, VEGETARIAN, VEGAN, RAW!

What started out as a simple wish to live healthier, to have more energy, and to teach my children, has for me evolved into a wondrous awareness and a true awakening and a vibrant and healthy lifestyle.

My journey with raw foods started as a mom of two amazingly beautiful boys. My dream for them was simple, to grow up being both happy AND healthy. I am sure this vision is the same for many moms. We start our journey with what we ourselves have been taught by our own mothers. But experience is the greatest teacher we have, and very quickly we come to understand that our journey is an evolution, ever changing, and as we learn new thoughts and ideas, we also gain new understanding in our life. These things cause us to pause and to re-evaluate the lessons we thought we knew.

Today, my boys are fourteen and sixteen, not really boys any longer, but now young men who are close to starting their own journeys. My dream for them built on health and happiness has now grown. I wish to teach them a harmony between life and nature, the ways in which to live and build a healthy lifestyle, and the beliefs in contributing not only to others but also to our environment.

UNDERSTANDING, THE FIRST STEP OF ACCEPTANCE

Green smoothies and juices, dehydrated fruits, twenty bananas a day… Is there really a way?

One of the biggest challenges I face daily in teaching my boys the benefits of a raw food diet comes from friends, family, teachers, and peers who simply do not understand the lifestyle. Often times, others simply want to share what they feel is "best" for one another, but judgment and disapproval are quickly attached to this way of life.

My oldest son is very fond of green smoothies, and once we discovered how easy it was to make this delicious drink, he made the decision to take a large container to school in the mornings, along with a salad and more fresh fruit for lunch.

First came the comments from teachers at lunch, that he did not have an appropriate meal, many offering suggestions to him of items that his mom might consider packing. Next were his peers, who, not being familiar with drinks that were brilliant green in color, made the choice to tease instead of talking. Now as a teen, peer pressure is already something that can be stressful in many ways without adding the attention of the neon smoothies. So, very quickly, bottles were purchased to "camouflage" the drinks inside. We are thankful that with some creative thought, we were able to navigate through many of these situations.

But every story must at some point have tales of positive affirmations. While sitting recently with my son at school, his counselor inquired as to his understanding of his health class. They were studying the "food pyramid." When asked if he had any questions regarding their study, he confidently replied, "No, my mom has taught me all I need to know regarding food!"

It's times like these that my heart soars and I know that my efforts are immeasurable!

THE PROTEIN AND HEALTH MYTH

"Let food be thy medicine and medicine be thy food"

– Hippocrates

In our society today, there are so many diets, fads, facts, trends, supplements, super-foods, medications, and information that one can easily become disenchanted with the idea of obtaining truly vibrant health.

The Protein Myth - How much protein do we ideally need?

Most of us have been raised with the notion that a lot of protein is good for us, that we need protein to grow up big and strong, but I ask you to ponder this: We are taught that, as infants, our mother's milk is the most perfect and ideal food. As an infant, there is no other time in our life when our growth is as dramatic. In our first year alone, we will quadruple in size and have more brain development than at any other time in our life. And just how much protein is in mothers' milk? The answer is surprising, ranging from 2.5 percent to 3.5 percent. Comparatively, the amount of protein found in cows' milk is 30 percent. So why do we believe we need either cows' milk or other forms of additional protein to be "healthy?" Have you ever heard of a health condition in which there was not enough protein? Simply, no, a condition such as this does not exist!

Today, the standard American diet (SAD) that many of us know consists of commercially produced and over-processed foods with genetically modified organisms (GMO's) that are deficient in enzymes, minerals, and nutrition. The basic fact is that our bodies are made up entirely of what we put into them; what we eat is reflected in our health and vitality. If we strive to live a healthy life, then simply stated, we must eat healthy food!

RAW HEALTH BENEFITS

"Body, Mind, and Spirit"

The philosophy and my belief behind a raw food lifestyle are both nutritional and spiritual in nature. It is really quite simple to understand that a diet comprised of live, living foods will provide us with a feeling of truly vibrant health, influencing every part of our life.

A basic belief for raw foodists is that life promotes life. Whole living foods contain a wide range of enzymes, vitamins and minerals, water, nutrients, and a powerful life force. Raw foods are the most abundant on the planet, and all living creatures, except for humans, eat their food in its natural, unaltered form. Nobody has to teach or train them how to eat, it is just instinctively known.

"You put a baby in a room with an apple and a rabbit.If it eats the rabbit and plays with the apple, I will buy you a new car!"

– Harvey Diamond

Eating raw is a way of life, a way to experience and support total wellbeing. Once you start to eat primarily organic raw, living foods, your quality of life will noticeably change. Increased energy, radiant and youthful skin, clear eyes, and a sound immune system can be easily felt, in addition to weight loss, as your body will gravitate to its natural state—Bliss!

When our bodies are fed with the optimal nutrition, we can easily enter into a deeply balanced state, with increased feelings of mental clarity, peace, and tranquility. Often we have a deeper understanding not only of one's self but also of those around us.

THE FOUR LIVING FOOD GROUPS

- **Raw Living Foods** represent the element of Water and are life giving!

Any food in its naturally RAW and vibrant, form such as fruits, vegetables, and fresh herbs.

- **Sprouted Foods** represent the element of Air and are cleansing and regenerative!

Any type of seed, nut, or grain that has been soaked to form a new plant, beginning with the sprout. Wheatgrass, alfalfa, buckwheat, and lentil sprouts are wonderful examples.

- **Cultured Foods** represent the element of Fire and are energizing and transformational!

These foods have had beneficial cultures introduced into them (bifidus, koji, and acidophilus). Some common known cultured foods are kombucha, miso, seed cheese, and kimchee.

- **Dehydrated Foods** represent the element of Earth and are very grounding and sustaining!

Dehydrated foods have had the water removed via a gentle drying at very low temperatures (less than 118 degrees).

Dried fruits and vegetables, crackers, breads, and herbs are great examples.

THE ART OF RAW LIVING

Remember, you are what you eat...

There is true beauty found in consuming foods fresh from the farm, garden, or tree that they grew upon. The closer you are to the source of harvest, the higher quality and more vital it is. Fresh, organic, and local foods (when available) are enchanting, delicious, and refreshing! The quality from these foods is easily noticed in our everyday health and well worth the investment in not only ourselves and but also in our communities. However, at times and in certain parts of the world, it is not as easy to buy fresh or local organic food. In cases of limited availability, there is a simple rule that one can use in choosing items, called "The Clean 15 and the Dirty Dozen." When choosing fruits and greens, items that can be purchased non-organically are things that are peeled in order to eat. Items such as bananas, melons, and avocado are safer to buy this way. However, items that you eat in their entirety, such as berries, greens, apples, and celery are better purchased organic.

There is a conscious environmental shift taking place on our planet today, and there has never been a more important time to incorporate a raw food lifestyle. Whether you are just discovering the joys of raw food, or you are experienced in the raw lifestyle, we share a common journey of transformation.

Just by choosing to eat naturally, we can each contribute to the living raw health movement..."Body, Mind, and Spirit."

Beth Martens

Voice-liberating, Archetype, and Business Coach; Rebel-Mantra Singer: Mom: and Cancer Survivor

Beth tells the naked truth to help women entrepreneurs and creatives get past their marketing "butterflies," so they can fearlessly express their authentic voice to their ideal network and build empowered communities. Beth opens the door for change agents to take their lifework to the next level by helping them communicate their value (online and off), for more impact. Her transformational archetype readings reveal how women can connect and market with an authentic voice, make money sacred, and breathe the life into their dreams.

- www.bethmartens.com
- www.facebook.com/beth.martens.finding.your.voice
- www.twitter.com/bethmartens
- www.pinterest.com/bethmartens1
- ca.linkedin.com/pub/beth-martens/15/a70/71b/

LESSON 24

Seven Reasons Your Kids are Going to Thank You for Being Fully Self-Expressed and Valued for Your Life Work

By Beth Martens

~~~

Mothering is a divine role, with a lot of rewards, but it includes a great deal of sacrifice. I'm grateful I had my son at thirty-nine, but no matter how much you have already lived, the unrelenting call of the soul is to grow, expand, and express.

While carrying the heavy demands of mothering, that soul's voice is rather inconvenient. So many moms resort to living through their children and sacrifice their own personal development in "service" to their kids. But in case you think you are doing your kids a favor by putting off having an authentic voice in your life work, you're not.

To inspire you to go the extra distance, here are the seven ways your kids are going to thank you for taking risks with your voice.

1. YOU WILL LEAD THEM POWERFULLY BY EXAMPLE

Kids do as they see, not as we say. So, living by example is the most powerful way to teach your children they can have the soul-level satisfaction you experience when you are fearlessly expressing.

We all hope our kids are going to be creative, inspired, and be able to manifest their dreams. And it's so easy to want it for our kids, that we sacrifice doing it for ourselves in lieu of the next generation.

But the reality is, when your kids get to do something that you want for yourself, or you use them as an excuse not to get on with your own dreams, you are going to experience resentment. If you really want to make the biggest sacrifice for your kids, shout from the rooftops about your creative magic, be of service in your true vision, and have a voice for what you want to see grow in the world. Rest assured, your prodigy will be more likely to follow suit and do it for themselves, too.

2. THEY WILL ENJOY THE SPIN-OFF OF THE SYNCHRONICITY YOU CREATE FOR YOURSELF

What I've noticed from being self-employed in my heart's desires for more than a decade, and from coaching with women, is that when you express your authentic voice in your life purpose, you create synchronicity. And if you're in the flow, everyone around you gets to bask is in the flow, too.

When we resist offering the world the naked truth of who we are, the Universe tends to appear as if it is holding us back...even hostage. Why? Because we are destined for unbridled, full self-expression, and anything less is going to be some version of misery.

In its most extreme case, a lack of flow and synchronicity are going to express as disease. As a cancer survivor of more than a decade, I know the costs of not aligning with my authentic voice.

It is never too late to pick up the thread of what you are wired to express. And I'm not saying that to make you feel OK about putting it off, but to say your soul's voice is never going to be silent.

3. YOU WILL BE EXPONENTIALLY HAPPIER WHEN YOU GIVE IN SERVICE

By being in the pocket of your life purpose and its voice, you will make enough money to spend more quality time with your children!

Money does not buy happiness, but without it, your ability to create the lifestyle you need to be satisfied is diminished. Being empowered to hire out some of the mundane tasks of the daily life can be the biggest blessing and takes tension and stress off of our plates.

And trumping all of the conveniences of a better lifestyle, your sense of satisfaction with your lifework simply makes you a happier person. And a happy mom is a kid's big dream.

4. YOU WILL HANDLE REGRETS ON BEHALF OF YOUR FUTURE SELF AND SPARE YOUR KIDS THE PAIN OF WATCHING YOU DIE WITH YOUR BEST STUFF IN YOU

By taking the most challenging risks—where your soul has the most at stake—you will have no regrets on your deathbed. Having no regrets is good news for your children, who will likely survive you. I know, I've been there, on my deathbed with a stage 4 lymphoma and seen firsthand what I was going to regret.

Through applying your conscious awareness this way, these future regrets can be dealt with and avoided. So I often ask myself and my clients, "What are you going to regret at the end of your life?"

Here are the top 5 on my list of regrets when I was facing what could have been the end of my life:

1. My creative projects were not finished.

2. I hadn't expressed unbridled love.

3. I had let fear stop me from totally being myself.

4. I spent time working for money, instead of for happiness and the greater good.

5. I took for granted the people I love and who love me.

5. YOUR KIDS WILL FEEL MORE SAFE

When you have a strong voice for yourself and stand up for your truth, you will also become a stronger voice for your children. In this confidence, you will stand up for your kids when it matters and create security in them—that they belong to a community that cares.

Kids need champions to maintain their innocence and honest vulnerability, and your powerful voice is going to give them the sense of being safe in the world.

They will learn to see their voice as a powerful, natural resource to which they can turn when they need that security, a sense of their own authority, and when they are getting ready to be pillars of safety and security for those weaker than them, too.

6. YOU WILL HAVE PLEASURE IN YOUR WORK AND THEREBY GIVE YOUR KIDS UNENDING HOPE FOR THE WORLD

Expressing authentically from your core, and enjoying the rewards of that both financially and in the results of your lifework, it will give you deep pleasure and satisfaction. Pleasure and joy are not the luxuries of life, because children need to feel like the world is a truly hopeful place—where they can play and create what they feel is in their heart and souls.

While I was struggling for my life with cancer, I experienced pleasure through my many creative channels. Despite physical limitations, joy shined through the storm of illness, treatments, and constant losses, and helped me recover against the odds.

And as a mother, pleasure is more important than ever. Because when I'm joyful and satisfied by my life, I'm pleased (not just obligated) to provide my family the life they need and want.

7. YOU WILL CREATE HEALTHY COMMUNITY WHERE THE NEXT GENERATION WILL THRIVE

Being a beacon of your inner most desires and vision for how you can contribute your gifts to the world is the most beautiful and organic way to attract your tribe. By the word "tribe," I mean those beings that will not only get you but those who will want to be part of the excitement you create and to see the possibilities through your eyes.

We are clearly here to help each other. And it's my sense that the "play of life" includes that we are not going to be able to do anything exceptional (which all callings are) without the input, support, and inspiration of many. Expressing fearlessly means that those who are in alignment with you can easily find you. And it also means the naysayers will want to get further away from you. And that will save you a lot of time you can devote to enjoying your kids.

Kids don't just need a mom, or a mom and a dad. They need a whole organic mess of examples, of voices and personalities to put together the stuff of who they are. When you raise children in community, they will thank you for inheriting an interwoven web of possibilities that transcend the limitations that any one caregiver may have, and they'll see how interdependence becomes the glue that keeps us compelled to do our part and contribute to the greater good of all.

In closing, there are nearly endless ways your kids will thank you for being self-expressed and valued for your lifework. But with these seven points in mind, take a minute and look at the reasons you may put it off and see if it outweighs the benefits of leading by example, enjoying greater synchronicity, greater happiness, avoiding future regrets, creating a feeling of security and safety, healthy pleasure, and strong community.

When you are putting your genuine goodness out into the world, playing with your lifework, creating something amazing from nothing, and being valued for it, you inherit them the missing link—hope!

Jacqueline Allen

Jacqueline created Dynamic Health Consulting in 2013. She's a yoga instructor, Board Certified Holistic Health Practitioner, and member of the American Association of Drugless Practitioners. In 2001, she created The Path Work for Conscious Living, a healing arts counseling business that focuses on the concept of spirituality being maturation of the personality, hands on healing techniques, chakra balancing and restructuring, clearing childhood wounds, working with defenses, character structures, and relationships. She's a Reiki Master and Minister, having performed many weddings. Living with her beloved Jack, she spends quality time with her grandchildren, enjoying the Great Northwest lifestyle, where she was born and raised.

✉ Jacqueline@dynamichealthconsuling.com

🏠 www.DynamicHealthConsulting.com

🏠 www.pangeaorganics.com/sites/jacquelineallen

f www.facebook.com/dynamichealthconsulting

🐦 www.twitter.com/dynamichealth2U

📞 253 606 2937

LESSON 25

Out of Chaos Comes Organization

By Jacqueline Allen

~~~~

We all breathe.

From that first autonomous act, to our final letting go, we breathe our way through every moment that is our life. Deeply, as we prepare for enormous effort, or a short, shallow pant, as we steer a course through pain and fear, our inhalations pace the ecstasies of love, and the tragedies of loss, binding exhilaration to sorrow, down through the thread of our lives.

Mom and dad were first-time parents when I was born. They made their best effort to provide for me and my three sisters. Mom was the "Martha Stewart" of our day. Everything was in its place, organized, clean, and pretty. Born first, I was a leader by design. "Don't do it unless you do it right," he'd say. "Open and close that door quietly one hundred times until you learn not to slam it." "Be Perfect," is what I heard.

Dad was a Master Finish Carpenter. One day, he got ill and an ambulance came to the house. He was taken away and didn't come back for a month. Instantly, our world and perfect family was shattered. At thirty-two, he had a debilitating stroke. He was never the same again. Somewhat disfigured, he looked like a monster to me, at twelve. Eventually, he became one of the first men to receive a pacemaker. I witnessed his arduous effort to learn again to walk, to talk, to write, and develop his motor skills; everything we took for granted. It was clear life was not going to be like the picture I had held in my imagination. A new picture was slowly emerging, and with patience, perseverance, and love, we would get through this. I just needed to let go of the outcome. I trusted we would be alright, even though our breadwinner was no longer able to provide for us. At that time, there was no welfare or public assistance. Mom never worked outside the home, or learned to drive. I remember feeling so scared for my parents. How were we going to survive? What was happening to our family? I witnessed as my dad never gave up, having hope, working so hard to come back. He was determined to see his children grow and to see his grandchildren. He built the fireplace in our home one brick at a time. Each brick was a struggle, but he did it.

For him, it was one day at a time, one task at a time. Dad instilled in me that if I put my mind to it, I could do anything! His mantra was, "Don't think about it, just do it." I thought it was so ironic when NIKE later came out with the slogan "Just do it." When things at home settled down, I was introduced to gymnastics. I always loved swinging on the ropes and playing on the monkey bars dad had built for us girls. Along with my horse, this had become my way of releasing stress as a young girl. I did become a gymnast, and with six years of dedicated, focused intention, I became the captain of the high school team, and a state champion.

Within two years of graduating from high school, I became a first-time parent. What an event, a challenge, and rewarding experience. In all, I was blessed with four sons, from three pregnancies. The second and third were twins. Talk about chaos. My early life lessons kicked into high gear. Thankfully, Mom was there to guide me with my firstborn, and later, with the twins. She helped me establish consistent schedules that provided the structure I surely needed, but I still felt so overwhelmed. I will never forget that day when I was at the doctor's office with the four-month-old twins.

The wise family nurse took me aside and said, "Jacqueline, there is always tomorrow, don't feel like you have to do it all today." Wow! This was exactly what I needed to hear. I was given permission to take care of myself. Today we call it "self-care." What could this mean for me? While the boys napped, I would exercise in front of the television with fitness guru, Jack LaLanne. Then, I started practicing gymnastics again at the local community college. I dreamt of doing gymnastics in my sleep. My body was speaking to me, and I was listening. It was a breath of fresh air.

As the three boys grew, there were many demands and many changes in our lives, including another brother. How was I going to continue managing the chaos? I can tell you it was no bed of roses raising four sons. It's been my greatest challenge. Balancing everything else has been delicate. I became real good at thinking ten steps ahead, always being prepared, organized, and ready for every situation.

Like you, I've had my share of life-changing events. My husband changed jobs and we moved from a beautiful new home in the community where I was raised into a neighborhood that was not where I would have chosen for my boys, that I knew nothing about. Within three years, my oldest son ran away, and by sixteen, had his first of five children. I was a grandmother at thirty-five and still raising my boys. Life was stressful, and after considerable counseling, my husband and I eventually divorced. It took a great leap of faith to end that relationship and to trust that I could be successful in creating a new business. I'd been married for seventeen years and never worked outside the home or taken a college course. My foundation from childhood came to the forefront once again. I trusted that if I focused, and set my intention, that I could do whatever I put my mind to. In time, my business venture was a statewide operation, and I was in the top 6 percent of income for women. I was a proud Momma.

As the boys grew older, athletics and family sports were at the center of our activities. Again, this seemed to be the common thread in our lives for structure and stress reduction. As a result, they learned to be dependable, cooperative, on time, compassionate, competitive, yet were good sports. Today, a great deal of our time goes toward supporting our grandchildren's athletic endeavors. We have an eight year old that's well on her way to becoming a successful gymnast.

As busy moms, how can we create and maintain a happy lifestyle when it is continually evolving and challenging us? How do we consistently manage stress? Throughout life, paths unfold that can set us on a course for ease and peace of mind. I was thirty-eight when I was introduced to yoga. It's been my focus and inspiration. It reminds me of the mind-body connection that is so prevalent in gymnastics. Yoga relieved the pain in my body and tension in my back and shoulders from years of hard work, primarily because of the practice of the yogic breath. Breath is Prana; literally, it is our life-force energy. The breath is our connection to Spirit—all that is. Breathing from our diaphragm, we oxygenate the blood 80 percent more than by breathing from the upper chest. The breath opens channels in our body that help facilitate the healing response. I loved yoga so much I became a Certified Yoga Instructor and have been teaching now for eighteen years, helping others with their self-care. I would like to close with this meditation that I often include during class. It opens the heart and facilitates the healing response in the mind, body, and spirit.

Sitting or lying, inhale slowly through the nose, expanding your lower abdomen as if it were a balloon, to a slow count of seven. Exhale, pulling the belly in toward the spine, counting to nine. As you become more relaxed, bring your attention to the heart center, feeling your heart beat. Now feel the love of a child, or pet, or a place that makes you feel happy and joyful. As you visualize and evoke this loving vibration, feel your heart start to glow and radiate healing energy. Visualize this energy flowing through your veins, into your muscles, tendons, organs, and cells. Bathe in this energy; stay here as long as you like. When you feel the fullness of this loving, healing vibration, extend it outward to a loved one. Now send this energy out into your community and around the world. Visualize all living things and the planet being healed, and see everyone for who we truly are—Happy, Healthy, and Holy.

May we learn to breathe not only days, but moments, filled with joy. And as we do, may we remember long that to breathe is to inspire.

Namaste, Jacqueline Allen

Angelica-Lee Aspiras-Liristis

Angelica-Lee Aspiras-Liristis is a Certified Holistic Health Coach and Reiki Master. As the creator of Journey True Holistic Health Coaching, Angelica customizes health and wellness programs for groups and individual clients. She received her holistic education from the Institute of Integrative Nutrition and is certified by A.A.D.P. Before the birth of her son, Angelica worked as an actress, performing on Broadway, Off-Broadway, with national tours, and on television. She earned her bachelor's degree from the School of Music at FSU. It is with great joy and gratitude that she is adding "writer" to her repertoire of titles! "Love and Gratitude to my family, especially to Michael and Gabriel!"

✉ Journeytruehealth@gmail.com

🏠 www.JourneyTrue.com

f www.facebook.com/JTrueholistic

🐦 www.twitter.com/GeliTrue

Body Miraculous: Be Empowered!

By Angelica-Lee Aspiras-Liristis

~~~

"Is that a pancake?!"I've discovered yesterday's breakfast under my oven drawer while attempting a kitchen floor mini-workout as we wait for the oatmeal to bubble. Gabriel picks up the discarded piece and aims for my mouth, dropping it down my shirt instead.

"YIAAAAAAAAAAAAH!"He claps in an operatic victory, pleased to share his day-old breakfast with Mama. I'm more amused than squeamish, regardless of the fact that I have a large bite of buckwheat lost in my camisole. We have at least three more minutes for the oatmeal—plenty of time for an impromptu dance party/beat box tutorial. I'm partial to my new all-time favorite audience of one. Though in reality, he has become *my* favorite show!

This is a typical Saturday morning with Gabe.

It was pretty spectacular when I figured out how to integrate workouts into playtime, and "me time" into this new version of life. As mothers, we all know the value of a break once in a while—self-care is a necessity!

Your body *is* miraculous! It is the divine temple in which your vibrant spirit resides; the "mother ship" from whence your beautiful children were created and nourished, and one of the most ingenious living machines in the history of all creation. As a mom, your most vital resource available is your body, and all the intricate systems collaborating within it. Taking time to nourish and maintain it should not be perceived as a well-deserved luxury, reserved only for the every-so-often. To neglect your own aching muscles, to ignore stiffened joints, and to deem your own radiance undeserving and unimportant

176

is to devalue your own Grace. Most importantly, when you forget to love and care for your own body, it will lose its ability to serve you at the supreme level that is necessary for keeping up with the needs of your precious family.

When you start feeling run down, out of focus, or under the weather, that is the time when your body is shouting, "Hey, Lady! Love me too, PLEASE!"

Adequate sleep (Truly, this means eight hours, but for most, it's anything past the two hour mark!), proper hydration (eight to ten glasses of water a day), and a nutrient-dense diet (with whole, unprocessed foods) are all key facets of a healthy plan. Nutrition, hydration, and meditation are what I like to refer to as the internal elements for self-care. When these are employed regularly, the benefits are first processed within you and then develop outward. Like a rose pulling water and minerals through the soil, from roots to each gilded leaf and petal, all living things require the assimilation of the proper energy (food, water, rest, and release) to thrive and serve in the full beauty for which they were created.

External elements are of equal importance. Physical activity is paramount! Exercise is not just about losing baby weight. Of course, we all want to feel gorgeous and slide into our favorite pair of jeans. It is not such a mystery that a strong and healthy body is a lovely thing, both to behold and to be! Not to stray too far from the immediate point, but let's establish that you are ALL beautiful (inspiring, courageous, and powerful) already and evermore. It is so important that we remember that, especially when it comes to our physical form.

Self-care is all about taking action from a place of love and worthiness, not an act of frustration against the body that carries you through life. You are the boss! Be inspired as you discover how to make motion a part of your life in forms that bring you joy. Before my son, I loved Bikram yoga, kickboxing, dance, and extreme classes. I look forward to returning to those in the future, but like many moms, I now have a harder time getting away for fitness routines. If this sounds familiar to you, there are many options for enjoyable workouts at home, and for little to no cost. Yes, without expensive memberships or class fees, you can still boost your metabolism, tone muscles, and pump up your cardiovascular and lymphatic systems.

You can use workout DVDs, or even tune into the fitness channel if you have cable. My new favorite workout is playing with my son. After an hour of chasing, dancing, and carrying around my twenty-five-pound "airplane," every muscle in my body has been worked to the maximum! Who knew that playtime could be so productive? Of course, the simplest way to a healthy and happier body is actually walking, believe it or not. Plain old walking at a brisk pace, through your neighborhood, inside on a treadmill if you have one, outside with your kids, or around your house. You could even get an inexpensive pedometer to track your steps. Ideally, you want to aim for 10,000 steps a day, but just get your body moving!

Now, I want to go back a little bit to revisit the lymphatic system and highlight the leading role it plays in our overall health, weight retention, and even the appearance of skin, including the tone, elasticity, and texture. The lymphatic system is the complex internal pathway that serves as a one-way drainage system for lymph—the carrier fluid that transports all the toxins, waste, and any other undesirables extracted from the food we consume, and the pollutants, bacterium and viruses we are exposed to. There are more than seven hundred lymph nodes distributed throughout this system. These chambers contain lymphocytes—superhero cells that exist to devour and filter out all of the aforementioned maladies. Without proper circulation of the lymph fluid, this process is compromised. You may feel heavy and fatigued. Sore lymph nodes begin to swell and your joints may ache. Skin will look and feel puffy, and cellulite seems more visible. These are all signs of stagnation in your body's drainage system.

Unlike our cardiovascular system, which is constantly working to cleanse our blood with every heartbeat, the lymphatic system's sole source of motion is dependent upon our daily movement and deep breathing. In addition to regular exercise, you can greatly improve your circulation through lymphatic massage, body brushing/body scrubs, and detoxifying seaweed baths. That's right. That delightful deep tissue massage and stress-melting effleurage is good for you. Tossing some iodine rich bladderwrack into a hot tub of water can tone sagging skin. With the use of a simple salt scrub or natural bristle body brush twice a week, you can simultaneously achieve dimple-free, glowing skin and assist your body's natural renewal process. Healthy habits sustain a beautiful body!

This does not have to be a grandiose production that monopolizes hours on end. If you have the freedom to leave the house for a run (or a class), or can budget for a spa day, then that is fantastic! Your health and well-being are essential to your own efficiency, and there is no room for guilt when it comes to responding to the cues your body is sending out. If getting away is simply not an option, do not despair. I too am a self-employed, stay-at-home mama, and I wholeheartedly relate to you! Therefore, below is one of my favorite basic remedies: the classic Salt Glow. The instructions are simple and the ingredients are inexpensive and easy to find online, or in your local health food store. I hope this has inspired your total body regimen—Now get GLOWING!

Salt Glow Scrub

Ingredients:

- 2 cups Fine-Grain Sea Salt

- 1 cup Light Carrier Oil (almond, grapeseed, or jojoba are wonderful)

- Favorite Essential Oil

- Mixing Spoon

- Medium Mixing Bowl

- Mason Jar (or other waterproof container with a lid)

Instructions:

In a medium-sized mixing bowl, combine 2 cups of fine-grain sea salt with one cup of your chosen oil. Mix these together until the oil is evenly soaked into the salt. For an aromatherapy infused scrub, you may add 3-4 drops of essential oils and then stir the salts well. Pour your scrub into a re-sealable container and you are ready to go.

How to use:

For best results, and most effective lymphatic stimulation, apply the scrub as you would do a "dry brushing" therapy. Before bathing, beginning with the soles of the feet, apply your scrub in a circular motion, gently sweeping upwards. Beware of the oil on your feet. You may wish to sit on the edge of your bathtub at first, so you don't slip. Continue with this application in the direction of your lymphatic flow, moving up the legs and torso towards the heart with the same light sweeping motion, adding more of the scrub when needed. Repeat the application on both hands, starting at the fingertips, moving to the palms and continuing up and under the arms, over the shoulders, and ending at the heart.

After the scrub is applied, you can relax in a warm bath or shower as usual. Be sure to use a good moisturizer immediately after you towel off. This will lock in the moisture for baby softness. Enjoy your radiant new skin and be thankful for your miraculous body!

Krista Gustavson

Krista Gustavson is a Certified Holistic Wellness Coach and Facilitator who specializes in detox for mind, body, and soul. She is the founder and co-creator of "Empowering a Woman's Soul" retreats. Krista inspires women to illuminate their beauty and nourish their body and soul in the most fun and natural way.

She is a conscious mother of three girls, who she believes are her greatest life teachers.

Krista empowers mothers to become whole, beautiful, and complete without depriving themselves, so they can live in Bliss!

🏠 www.rawbeautywellness.com/hotmama

🅕 www.facebook.com/rawbeautywellness

🐦 www.twitter.com/kristagustavson

LESSON 27

Hot Mama's Detox for Life — Living in Bliss

By Krista Gustavson

~~~

From the very first day we become Mamas, it's as if we get lost in time. We become absorbed with our little beings. Nurturing others comes naturally for us. Mamas feel guilty for taking even a moment for ourselves. I came to a place in my life after a broken down marriage, going through the motions of being a single mama, that left me completely depleted. In 2010, I had nothing left to give. During that time, I tapped into my soul and awakened. It changed my whole life!

I became aware that I had forgotten to nurture myself. It was a pivotal moment in my life where I recognized it was time to honor my body and soul.

It began with the power of nutrition, but it was detoxing that led me on an inspiring, transformational journey that would change my life forever! It was the missing piece to becoming whole, beautiful, and complete.

Many Mamas feel they would be depriving themselves with a detox, but what if the foods that aren't fueling your body and the stress you get to let go of is everything that has been keeping you from stepping into your Hot Mama self?

Temporary discomfort speeds up your body's healing process. Detoxing allows one to be more in tune with their body than ever before and will give you a deeper understanding of the foods that fuel you the most. You will feel lighter and more joyful.

The body detoxes in several different ways. It's the body's natural process to rid unwanted toxins that cause pain, inflammation, and dis-ease. One thing I learned is having a support system in place through the detox process is vital, because it requires us to change.

Detoxing the body gives us an opportunity to cleanse our mind and emotions, letting go so we can heal old, buried patterns that cause dis-ease. Because our body lives in the past, it can take several months to heal a condition. Our natural response is to hold onto everything. Detoxing seasonally will nourish your body while feeding your soul.

The temporary discomfort the first time I detoxed was worth the empowering result I experienced. I developed a deeper relationship with my body and fell in love with myself.

As I began to change, I noticed that I was thriving more the ever. Being in my body, beauty was radiating like never before.

HOW DOES DETOX WORK?

Detox is about eliminating foods that may be wreaking havoc on your system, giving your body time to rest and reset, and letting go of non-food toxins that do not contribute to your body. Detox increases energy, enhances your health and wellbeing so you feel vibrant, and supports deep healing and recovery from dis-ease. You'll discover that the healing process will nourish, heal, and transform your life inside and out.

Why detox? The most important reason is to increase vitality, build new cells, reduce inflammation, and eliminate unwanted toxins that build up in the body that cause dis-ease.

Every food you consume, every breath you inhale, and everything you touch during your day brings with it contaminants. This forces the liver to work hard at detoxifying your body. Because there is no way to avoid all of these toxins, they build up and our bodies have to work even harder to process them. This causes the body to go into overload.

Digestion is related to so many different health problems. Supporting proper digestion is the key element to weight loss and –dis-ease prevention. For metabolism to function normally, your system must be free of toxicity.

A detox is a great way to kick-start any health program, such as weight loss. It rejuvenates the liver and rids the body of yeast. The Hot Mama Detox for Life is a total body experience that combines the physical, spiritual, mental, and emotional elements to our being.

Here are **2 types of toxins you should be aware of:**

1. Exotoxins come from sources outside of the body, such as pesticides, inhalants, foods, drugs, body products, and cleaning products.

2. Endotoxins come from sources inside of the body, such as metabolic by-products, hormonal overload, free radicals, and toxic emotions.

HOT MAMA DETOX - SIMPLE STEPS TO GETTING STARTED

Begin by gradually eliminating animal protein and all processed foods, including refined sugar, dairy, and wheat. You'll want to add in whole foods: a variety of in-season, local, preferably organic fruit and vegetables.

Supplementation such as **probiotics** is a compound of two Greek words: "pro" to signify promotion of, and "biotic," which means life. Probiotics give you the essentials for life, with good bacteria.

Juicing allows you to get the most nutrients while giving your body a break because it allows for easy digestion, which is easier on the body. Juicing allows you to heal on a cellular level. Your body will receive more nutrients than ever! With juicing, you are cleansing the body's entire system. I love a fresh raw juice of 4 carrots, 1 apple, 1 beet, 1/4 lemon, and a pinch of ginger.

Children love juicing too but may prefer something fruity: 1 apple, 1 orange, 1 pear, 2 celery stalks, and 1/2 lemon. Smoothies are another great way to get a variety of nutrients your body requires, including a variety of super-foods. Having a smoothie every morning is a great way to kick-start your day!

Exercise aids in the release of toxins. It stimulates the nervous system and releases endorphins into the body. Exercising because you feel you have to becomes work. Choose something to get your body moving in a way that you love so it feels good. You'll find you can't live without it!

Another important element to detox is hydration. Getting enough water will help flush toxins out of your body. Your target is to drink 1/2 your weight in ounces every day.

A daily ritual is essential for peace of mind. A ritual could include walking, meditation, yoga, or some other form of relaxing your body, combined with self-care, to provide stillness and tranquility. This is the most important element to reducing stress.

DETOXING YOUR MIND AND EMOTIONS – LIVING IN BLISS

The second phase of the Hot Mama's Detox is: whatever's good for your soul, do that!

Acknowledge yourself as a beautiful being. My simple tools will help clear your mind, which is vital to a healthy body.

Awareness is the key to everything. Letting go of the thoughts, feelings, and emotions that hold us back in life brings us to a state of tranquility. When we are fully aware, we are conscious with the space to understand what we are truly experiencing in the moment.

Bring your attention to your body and notice if there is any pain or discomfort. Do you feel energized or tired? Don't go into judgment about it, just notice it.

Acknowledging what we feel in the moment is awareness.

Being present is the most valuable gift you can give to yourself and others. This can be a challenge for Mamas, as we are often so distracted.

We get so busy with daily tasks that it can be difficult to find time to be aware and present because we are living in our mind. Often, we are not fully in our body because of this.

Choose something every day that is fun or relaxing to get out of "always doing" and more "BEing" in your body.

Do you make choices with joy? You know the feeling we get when we have to do something? It feels heavy! The next time you have a choice to make about home, kids, health, or your job, choose only for YOU! Honor yourself by choosing what feels light. You create more joy for yourself and your family this way. Notice how joy feels in your mind and body. This is what I call "living in Bliss," because when you choose what's true for you, you raise your vibration so you are centered in your body and you can heal faster.

When we take the time to nourish ourselves, we have more energy to give to our families.

A simple walk every day, snuggling up with a great book, having a bath by candlelight, yoga at the beach, writing, or any other kind of ritual that calms you. Honoring yourself each day brings a feeling of tranquility into your life so you feel special.

When I discovered how to BE in my body and integrate the power of detox into my own life, being a Mama became so much more fun—less work, less stress! When your children see you taking time to nourish yourself, they learn to respect the time you are choosing for you. No more guilt! You're naturally showing them how to honor themselves. When we are joyful and living with ease, we are vibrant, healthy, and living in Bliss. Are you ready to step into your Hot Mama?

Tara Kennedy-Kline

Tara Kennedy-Kline is a certified family parenting expert and popular radio and TV personality, best known as the acclaimed author of *Stop Raising Einstein: Discover The Unique Brilliance In Your Child… and You* and *The Problem with Kids…is Parents!* Tara redirects parents who are trying to raise the perfect child in an imperfect world and inspires them to discover the unique brilliance in their children and themselves. Her approach steers away from attempting to achieve perfection, and instead, choosing to embrace a life filled with potential and possibilities for children and their parents.

You can connect with Tara on all the social media outlets by visiting her website:

⌂ www.tarakennedykline.com

The Genius is in the Balance

By Tara Kennedy-Kline

~~~

My youngest son, Alex, used to write brilliant stories. Scratch that. Alex used to tell brilliant stories. His father and I were given the distinct honor of writing them down for him…but he doesn't even do that very much anymore.

Even though he is nearly thirteen years old, has an IQ of 143, and attends a mainstream 7th grade classroom, Alex has actually lost his ability to write stories during his third grade year. At least, that's the public school system's version of things.

The truth is, Alex hasn't lost the ability to write. What he has lost was the passion—the desire and the courage to write the way he once did. The reason for that is simple: instead of being celebrated for their unique storylines, colorful character development, and hysterical sidebars, his stories were edited for "acceptable content" and poorly graded for "missing essential data" based on the requirements of the rubric. I realized this fact recently when my husband and I attended a meeting with Alex's teachers. We meet several times a year because our son is autistic, and we are involved with his schooling (and like any parent of any child, we know what he is capable of if given the right motivators and accommodations).At this particular meeting, I requested a full list of things our son has failed/done wrong/not turned-in, as well as the teachers' documentation of his progress—to include exceptional things he has done in their classrooms. Once we began talking, it was sadly fascinating that none of teachers/administrators present were discussing his progress, only his failures. Did they not realize this shining star-of-a-child was not a number or a "test subject."

He is my son! My baby! How could they not see the greatness in him that I see? And, perhaps more importantly, how could they not see how much of his creative, funny, spritely little spirit was being lost in all their judgment?!

I decided to try a little experiment, and each time someone mentioned something negative, I would respond with a positive comment or lesson that I could see coming from their perception of his failures. It took a while for many of them to turn around, but eventually, the conversation turned from a highlight reel of Alex's collective mistakes into a brainstorming session on how we could help Alex to become successful in each of their classrooms.

Following the meeting, Alex began an extended break from school, and all of my kids were home for six days in a row. (Being snowed in with two teenaged boys is rough enough, but trying to keep them entertained without killing each other or going into a technology coma is enough to drive any parent insane!). What was needed was a balance of what I needed from them—make-up work for school and house chores, and what they wanted to do—gaming and fun activities. We made a list of responsibilities, and what happened next was nothing short of miraculous.

We realized that Alex had fifteen (yes, fifteen) assignments that he had not completed in the current quarter, and some of them were actually really fun—a PowerPoint presentation on *Phantom of the Opera*, a story about "My Life as a Mummy," and writing a fable about a creature they picked and researched.

We started with *Phantom*, and I tried to get him in the spirit by turning on the Broadway channel. We spent an entire evening listening to show tunes while we cooked and ate dinner and played games. Because of his newfound inspiration, he created a masterful *Phantom* PowerPoint, and later, he told us that he loved the story so much that he would like to see the musical for his birthday!

Next, we pulled up the details for his fable. We used our own pets to create a personality for Alex's creature. I watched as my creative, funny, whimsical Alex surfaced to write a ten-page, beautifully written fable about a Fisher (which is ironic, because they don't fish!) who is immediately judged by his new neighbors based on his appearance and blamed for something he would never do because they didn't take the time to get to know him (more irony? Yeah...I believe so). It was truly a family effort, with his dad helping in research and his brother and I helping in the graphic arts department. And it also opened the door for some amazing conversations about friends, school, manners, judgment, and honoring our strengths.

Over the course of the break, he completed quizzes and crossword puzzles, made up songs, and blazed through math facts like a crazy man! He also played Minecraft, went sledding, played on the ice, and helped make up dinner menus, built massive structures out of Legos, did science experiments in the kitchen, had dance parties, and told hundreds of jokes (many of them inappropriate—but who cares, we were laughing!). We even went so far as to scan and email some of the important work to his teachers so they could see we were really working! At the end of that break, we were exhausted and rested, sad to go back, and excited to share all we accomplished all at the same time. I sent my sons to school knowing they were proud of all they had done and anticipating the flood of kudos from their teachers. What I received were emails about grades and the explanations of why they were so low. "But hey, at least he didn't fail!" was what I read. "The fable was well-written but didn't meet the requirements of the rubric." "The crossword puzzle wasn't counted because, although he completed it, he didn't take it out of his folder and hand it in like the other students."

And then it hit me...Alex isn't failing, he is simply struggling, trying to fit all of his brilliance into such a tiny, restrictive mold. I wasn't serving him by making him fit, I was squashing his brilliance by making the mold the only guide! Then I remembered the inspiration for bringing the old Alex back: Following his lead, using those things he enjoys and is passionate about to inspire him to "get things done." Letting him learn from what he loves instead of trying to force him to love what he is being taught.

We had made the kitchen our laboratory with experiments like "Why do cakes rise?" and making spin art with milk, food coloring, and dish soap. We did math at the grocery store and by calculating how much he needed to get paid for chores if he wanted to buy that new PlayStation game. We studied the arts, history, and literature by reading, listening to and watching musicals and biographies about "the men who built America," and then taking a walk along the local train tracks. We had science class outside, discussing things like "thermal inertia" and why trees don't die when they lose their leaves. We accomplished all of it, AND because we laughed and had fun and didn't cram the info—but allowed it to happen organically—he'll remember it! He'll also remember so much more than simply the subject of those assignments. He gained skills in patience, accountability, sacrifice, and negotiation. He also learned commitment, appreciation, responsibility, and cooperation. And the value of bringing more of what you love and who you are into your work.

Of course, I'm not suggesting that we should stop sending him to school, or even ignore the lessons he learns from his teachers and the subjects they teach. But I AM suggesting that if we want our children to thrive, we must be willing to remove some of those extracurricular activities where someone who doesn't know them is coaching them to become masterful at something they don't like, and instead, spend that time exploring THEIR world and sharing OUR world with them. I want my sons and me to find a happy balance between life and learning, between homework and home life, between academia and adventure, life lessons and love of life. We need to be willing to let go of pushing them toward someone else's perception of perfection and allow them to bring more of what THEY love, their Unique Brilliance, into their space. When that happens, there is no such thing as failure, only higher learning! We would be amazed at our own—and our children's—genius and find greater peace and balance, if we just allowed ourselves to be passionate about and learn from those things we aren't graded on, and let life be the teacher.

Maureen Huntley

Maureen Huntley, CHHC, AADP. Maureen is the creator and founder of Mo Green Juice DBA, Vital Health for Life, LLC. Maureen gets her "green on" by juicing, bottling, selling, and distributing her green juices in NJ/NY (nationally soon!) via farmers markets, stores, and CSA's. Check Mo Green Juice at: www.mogreenjuice.com

Maureen has a BFA from Theatre School at DePaul University in Chicago and is a Certified Holistic Health Coach who has graduated from the Institute for Integrative Nutrition, accredited by Teachers College at Columbia University. Maureen is a certified L.E.A.N. educator, a member of the American Association of Drugless Practitioners, and holds additional certifications in Reflexology, Reiki, EFT, and Law of Attraction. Her training also includes vegan and raw foods chef certification through the Natural Kitchen Cooking School in Princeton, NJ. Maureen has studied with Alissa Cohen and is a certified Raw/Living Foods Chef.

 www.mogreenjuice.com

LESSON 29

MomZENse: A Juicy Journey

By Maureen Huntley

~~~

"The art of never making a mistake is crucial to motherhood. To be effective and to gain the respect she needs to function, a mother must have her children believe she has never engaged in sex, never made a bad decision, never caused her own mother a moment's anxiety, and was never a child."

– Erma Bombeck

Imagine if you will, close your eyes, take a deep breath, and feel a warm breeze, reminding you that you are in perfect alignment with the universe. You are taking such amazing care of yourself. Deep breath again. This tremendous feeling of calm strength and empowered energy moves all around you. Your health, weight, family, finances, career, home, and love life are exactly where you always dreamed they would be. Your children believe you are perfect. Your husband sees you as a goddess. Your dreams come true. Everything you think, do, and experience is in perfect harmony with your inner and outer being. Harmony is your mantra.

Ah…deep breath.

…Imagine if you will, close your eyes, take a deep breath, because **this** is your life. Ahhhhhh! You feel kind of chubby, tired, and angry that you're not taking better care of yourself, but how can you?! Your head is pounding, the children are screaming, the dog is barking. As you take a deeper breath, the smell of overflowing garbage wafts upward to your nose, as does the diaper pail in the furthest corner of your home. You have the tremendous feeling of being overwhelmed as the piles of laundry call out to you, the dishes are overflowing in the sink, the kids homework is all over the kitchen table, there are shoes and toys all over the floor, the bake sale cookies (gluten, dairy, and nut free with labeling) need to be made, and yet another dinner needs to get collected at the grocery store—oh, and the jewelry party you're hosting for a friend is tonight! Chaos has become your mantra. It has taken over your inner and outer being.

MomZENse, yes the Zen of Motherhood, is about taking that juicy journey of you within the chaos of life.

In the middle of my mothering chaos, the last thing I often remember to do is breathe, yet alone set a "healthy" intention and daydream about it. I often plod along, getting irritated along the way, feeling too exhausted to parent and too exhausted to care. Yet, what I know at my core is that I really need to take care of myself! If I don't take care of me, I can't take care of my family.

It starts with your breath. Take a deep breath. Tell your family to also.

FINDING MY MOMZENSE

Like so many women I know, I put all my attention on my family, my children, my husband, my parents, and extended family members. I am a take-charge woman! I am woman, hear me…cry. No one heard me as I slowly crumbled from the inside out. Here I stood on the edge of my life, trying to "fix" everyone but myself. I was so focused on what I fed them, what I let them watch, who they hung out with, and micro-managing life. Not only did I do it to my children and my husband, but I did it to my aging parents. If they did what I told them, I'd save them from the poor lifestyle choices they made. I was so busy managing everyone's health and wellbeing, that I had no time for myself. I was so concerned with what showed up in their behavior, attention, health, and yes, the toilet, but I was the one who was getting sick.

Standing in the kitchen with my father as I was lecturing him on health, I collapsed. My back went out and I went down. I couldn't move. The pain was beyond anything I'd ever experience, including labor and childbirth. It was a heck of an "aha" moment. In hindsight, it was the best thing that could have happened to me. It woke me up. It was my MomZENse moment. I needed to find the "ZENse" in this life of mine.

A JUICY JOURNEY

Getting a healthier family starts with a healthier you. It starts with what's going on in your brain and how it feels in your gut. The inner monologue that's been rambling on inside of you and how it makes you feel in your gut. Yes, that good ol' fashioned "gut feeling" — that feeling of right and wrong, good and bad, and how you feel it physically in your belly. What on earth have you been thinking? Really, what's going on in that pretty little head of yours? Stop and listen. Where is it showing up in your body, life, home, and your family?

What Juices up your life?

- Journal
- Draw
- Paint
- Run
- Sex
- Laugh
- Play
- Garden
- Decorate
- Go back to school
- Dream: _____

The future belongs to those who believe in the beauty of their dreams.

– *Eleanor Roosevelt*

Dreaming, we can change everything. It uplifts us, gives hope, ideas, and a vacation from the chaos. Every idea, invention, and solution began with an idea, a dream, and the belief it would come true.

The space to dream can seem so elusive. If we don't physically have the space, it's the lack of "mind" space, the chattering that takes up our brain, and life space. Even the chattering of all those around us, pulling, yanking…mom, mom, mom, mommy, mommy, MOM!!!!!

Time for a MomZENse time out.

JUICY INTENTIONS

- At bedtime, write down: five things I accomplished today, 5 things I am grateful for, and 5 things I intend to do tomorrow. Star the most important **self-love**. ALWAYS have a self-love on there.

Example: I intend to take the time to pluck my eyebrows today. (Hey, start small and work up if you need to). The goal is to work up to: I intend to look myself in the mirror every morning and acknowledge how beautiful my eyes are (or how beautiful, smart, funny… I am).

- When you awake, ALWAYS start with gratitude. Be grateful for the day and your process. Pick up your list, read it, and say out loud your intentions for this day.

- Segment intending: As you go through your day, bring awareness to how you go from one task to another. What are you thinking about? As you shift to different tasks, stop, take a deep breath, and ask yourself: "What is my intention in this situation?" Answer this and set your intention. Say it out loud, if you can.

Example: You're busy doing laundry and the phone rings. You run to get it and look at the caller ID. Take a deep breath. Ask yourself, "What is my intention as I pick up the phone?" Say out loud: "My intention with this call is to accomplish _____."

1. Don't forget to breathe. Breath is energy. Energy is what moves us forward in body, mind, and spirit. When you hold your breath, you stop intention, creation, and creativity. You were born to create creatively.

2. Get clear. Write it down as many times as you can and stick it on everything! (Post-it notes)

3. Share your intention with someone who is supportive and who will hold you accountable for taking action. Not with someone who you want/wish could support you when they never really have in the past. These non-supportive individuals are often those closest to us. They are in our lives as contrast to what we really want and need.

4. Celebrate that you did what you said you would do. Throw yourself a happy dance party, even if it's in your mind—nah, find the time to dance!

5. Be grateful for what you've accomplished! Tomorrow is another day of intentions to be set. You go, girl!

By setting intentions, you make it clear to yourself first. By setting intentions, you are creating your reality and not allowing the actions of others to dictate your choices.

EMPOWERING YOURSELF FORWARD FOR YOU!

Imagine if you will, close your eyes, take a deep breath, and feel a warm breeze, reminding you that you are in perfect alignment with the universe. You are taking such amazing care of yourself. Deep breath again. This tremendous feeling of calm, strength, and empowered energy moves all around you. Your health, weight, family, finances, career, home, and love life are exactly where you always dreamed they would be. Your children believe you are perfect. Your husband sees you as a goddess. Your dreams come true. Everything you think, do, and experience is in perfect harmony with your inner and outer being. Harmony is your mantra.

Ah…deep breath. All is possible.

Jennifer Leigh Burnett

Jennifer Leigh Burnett is a Certified Plant-Based Nutrition Coach and founder of Medicinal Nutrition. She helps women balance their Glow, Flow, and Hormones using healing whole foods. After being diagnosed with Hashimoto's Thyroid disease and suffering for years with dysmenorrhea, Jennifer balanced her symptoms holistically and rediscovered VIBRANT health. Her education encompasses over 150 dietary theories, integrating traditional philosophies, like macrobiotics and Ayurveda, with today's modern day nutrition concepts. She has studied at Cornell University, the State University of New York, and is a graduate of the Institute for Integrative Nutrition.

🏠 www.MedicinalNutrition.com

f www.facebook.com/MedicinalNutrition

🐦 www.twitter.com/NutritionTweet

𝓟 www.pinterest.com/HealingWithFood

📷 www.instagram.com/MedicinalNutrition

Happy Hormones for a Tranquil Life

By Jennifer Leigh Burnett, CHHC

~~~

Somewhere in the beautiful transition of motherhood, a once-peaceful lifestyle can feel as if it evaporated into sleepless nights, weight gain, irregular periods, dulling skin, and anxiousness. As a mother, you suddenly find yourself multi-tasking as caretaker, teacher, boo-boo mender, diaper changer, appointment setter, and chief of household. While a new and busier schedule certainly contributes to daily overwhelm, it is our hormones controlling just about everything behind the scenes. Women underestimate how much their hormones affect their everyday life. We attribute things like PMS, digestive imbalance, premature aging, decreased sex drive, emotional roller coasters, and mild depression as "things we are dealing with," but reality is, these could all be signs your hormones are calling out for help.

ANXIETY AND MOOD SWINGS

In a world where we are constantly on the go, our stress hormones are always in high demand. Stress of any kind calls upon the adrenal glands for help. The adrenals are walnut-sized glands located on the top of each kidney that act as important control centers for many of the body's hormones. Your adrenals don't care if you are late for work, stuck in traffic, didn't sleep well, mad at your partner, frustrated with your kids, or if you are face to face with a grizzly bear—they always respond the same way: by pumping out stress hormones. Constantly drawing upon our adrenals to balance an overloaded lifestyle can lead to cortisol imbalance, which is commonly associated with anxiety, quick-tempered reactions, lowered libido, an inability to concentrate, lowered immune function, and chronic fatigue. Unaware of what is happening with our hormones, we "power through" the day with extra caffeine and fake energy sources, which in turn exhausts our adrenals *even further*, creating a viscous cycle. Eventually, we may feel like we are running on fumes.

RESTLESS SLEEP AND INSOMNIA

When hormones are out of balance, one of the first noticeable signs is an inability to get to sleep, stay asleep, or sleep soundly. For some women, poor sleep could be related to a thyroid hormone imbalance, adrenal fatigue, or an imbalance of the sex hormones estrogen or progesterone. If sleeping is an ongoing and chronic issue, make sure you see your doctor to have these hormones tested. But no matter the cause of your sleepless nights, making key dietary changes, along with creating a sound sleep routine (outlined later in this chapter), will help to heal your body and re-establish healthy Z's.

ADULT ACNE, SUNSPOTS, AND PREMATURE AGING

Estrogen and progesterone, along with thyroid and a host of other hormones, help to balance the structure in your bones, the elasticity in your skin, the health of your heart, and much more. So when your hormone system starts to breakdown, your beauty may start to breakdown with it. Thinning hair, dull skin, sunspots, or an onset of adult cystic acne (commonly on the neck area) are just a few signs of a potential hormone imbalance. We all know there is no replacement for healthy glowing skin from the inside. So save your money, skip the beauty products, and heal *at the source* by evaluating the quality of your sleep, your water intake, and eliminating the unhealthy habits from your daily routine.

PAINFUL OR IRREGULAR PERIODS AND PMS

Irregular periods can mean different things for different women, but they are all rooted in hormonal imbalances. Some women experience missed periods, or periods that come and go. Others have a regular schedule but experience painful, heavy, and almost unbearable cycles. The root cause of irregular periods ranges from woman to woman. For me, I had a consistent 28-day cycle, but experienced heavy pain and discomfort to the point of debilitation (for decades). Until I began my path to healing with whole foods, I would visit doctor after doctor, each wanting to prescribe me "The Pill." After being spun in circles for years, and bottles of Advil later, I discovered the source of *my* painful periods were related to an autoimmune hypothyroid condition.

I want you to know that your menstrual cycle provides a wealth of information about your hormones, fertility, and total wellbeing. There are four phases of your cycle (Menstrual, Follicular, Ovulation, and Luteal phases) running continuously throughout your reproductive years, each delicately controlled by hormones. The more you understand your menstrual cycle, the more empowered you are about your hormonal health and can fully embrace your body's potential. Unless you *just* had a baby or are reaching menopause—irregular periods are *not* normal. Even if you had all the answers, DIET is the greatest contribution not only to our hormones, but to our whole-body health. To understand more about possible causes and action plans for irregular periods, as well as the four phases of your menstrual cycle, visit www.MedicinalNutrition.com/menstrualcycle.

Many women are plagued with PMS symptoms, which can include anxiety, breast tenderness, changes in appetite, mild depression, fatigue, fluid retention, irritability, and poor concentration. Women with high estrogen levels tend to have these same symptoms but with *much more* intensity. High estrogen levels can result from genetic, dietary, and environmental factors like endocrine disruptors in personal care products. I have found that women who *reduce* sugar, soy, gluten, and excessive animal proteins (including dairy) often experience a significant improvement in PMS symptoms over time.

YOUR HORMONE BALANCING ACTION PLAN.

We are what we eat. We've all heard it. But what we eat *quite literally* becomes who we are. The food we eat breaks down to fuel our blood, renews our cells, and even affects how we think and feel. I don't find it coincidental that in today's world we have reached epidemic levels of hormone imbalance parallel to a society addicted to diet trends, processed food, artificial flavors, sugar, fake sugar, and a dependence on medications. Your hormones are made from building blocks that require specific minerals, essential fatty acids, vitamins, and proteins (found in whole foods) to properly function. In the plan below, I give you ten expert tips to help you reclaim your hormonal health. I recommend trying one tip at a time, until you are comfortable with the lifestyle change, and then proceed to the next:

Build Bone Density with Dark Greens. When your estrogen production is low, you lose an average of 2%-4% of your bone strength with each passing year. Combat bone loss and boost bone density by consuming mineral rich, dark, leafy greens like kale, collards, and chards.

Boost Hormone Function with Coconut Oil. Coconut oil not only assists in balanced hormone production but aids with reducing inflammation, boosting metabolism, and promoting weight loss. It's antibacterial and antimicrobial properties are also excellent for boosting digestive and immune health.

Master Your Hormones with Maca. Maca is an adaptogenic root that aids in balancing overall hormones and assists in regulating estrogen levels. Maca is rich in energy boosting B vitamins, enzymes, essential amino acids, as well as bioavailable calcium and magnesium.

Blast PMS with Shatavari. Shatavari is one of the most rejuvenating herbs for women in Ayurvedic medicine. This herb helps to balance mood, combat PMS, reduce hot flashes, balance the reproductive system, and heal reproductive tissue.

Nourish the Nervous System with Valerian, Licorice, and Dandelion Roots Teas. Valerian root reduces stress on the nervous system, reduces anxiety, and helps to balance sleep cycles. Licorice root contains many anti-depressant compounds, great for reducing PMS and painful periods. Dandelion root is a natural detoxifier, packed with vitamins and minerals.

Boost Fertility and Energize with Royal Jelly. Royal Jelly is a great source of antioxidants, energy boosting B vitamins, amino acids, iron, and calcium. Excellent for anti-aging and boosting natural fertility. Add to teas, smoothies, or use as a supplement.

Holy Basil (also called Tulsi Tea). Tulsi tea has been called the "elixir of anti-aging." This mild tea has adaptogenic properties that naturally help to fight fatigue and stress, boost your immune function, and balance both hormone and blood sugar levels.

Magic Mineral Magnesium: Magnesium can relieve digestive issues, boost energy levels, quell anxiety, alleviate muscle spasms (including menstrual cramps), stop migraines, strengthen bones, reduce PMS, and much more. Some mineral rich, plant-powered foods include lentils, spinach, squash, pumpkin seeds, pasture raised eggs, sunflower seeds, avocados, almonds, and bananas.

Avoid Environmental Endocrine Disruptors. While we can't live in a bubble protecting us from every toxin on earth, you can take measurable steps to eliminate your toxic load. Plastics and parabens act as serious endocrine disruptors, interfering with healthy estrogen production and use in your body. Reduce and ELIMINATE your exposure by consciously avoiding canned foods, plastic drink containers, and personal care products that contain any sort of plastics, parabens, and phthalates.

Create a Sound Sleep Plan

To help promote a sound sleep, develop a simple plan of action by incorporating one or all of the below to your daily routine:

- Incorporate a night time tea ritual two hours before sleeping
- Choose sleep-promoting teas like lavender, chamomile, or valerian root
- Use a hot towel on your neck and face before resting
- Use essential oils to promote a tranquil sleep environment
- Write in a journal for five to ten minutes to empty buzzing thoughts from a busy day

When it comes to your endocrine system and your entire wellbeing, remember that we are self-healing organisms. When given half a chance, your body wants to rejuvenate, heal, and *thrive*. Take action today, one bite at a time, and always remember to consult with your doctor before incorporating any diet and lifestyle changes.

Conclusion

It is a great honor to present this book to all moms around the world. My intention is that every mom who reads this book finds laughter, inspiration, keys to succeed, comfort, and an excitement to continue the journey of the transformation in self, for herself, her spouse, her children, and community.

Becoming a mother is a natural part of life for some women. It is a very joyous gift of life. But it comes with big challenges. As a mother, it is a blessing to have a tribe of other mothers who support each other, help you when needed, and inspire you to become the best mom ever—beautiful mirrors.

This book is a full-balanced spectrum of areas to help Mom find healing in mind, body, and spirit. The word *balance* as a noun means an even distribution of weight, enabling someone or something to remain upright and steady; and balance as a verb means to keep or put something in a steady position so that it does not fall. I love the notation of balance enabling someone to remain upright and steady. Every co-author in this book helps Mom to rise up and step forward onto her path with a renewed outlook. We all worked day by day to formulate, consult, meditate, open, love one another, and strengthen each other in purpose of the vision—to complete this anthology for moms as a true go-to guide for inner tranquility.

I hope you enjoy every page, every message, and every co-author; so much that you will read it over and over again. I hope that you will take initiative to prevent disease and enrich your lifestyle with a child's heart and a mature mind. Never forget that change comes from within, and you are not alone on this journey. I hope that you can learn to love with all your might, and when you run empty, you will fill your cup as soon as you can with more love for yourself, for your spouse, and for your children.

Love, Light, and Blessings!

Join Our Tribe

Are you committed heart and soul to making necessary, permanent changes to your health and your family's health? Do you need support and a vehicle for change and awareness? Do you need coaching and support for diet and lifestyle changes, parenting, love, relationships, spirituality, intimacy, and career? Would you like to join a tribe of other likeminded moms working through a process of healing, complete wellness, and life fulfillment? Let us help you become fully awake in life. Move through mindset limitations and find your bold inner strength to persevere through life challenges and relationships. Become the best mom ever with support from likeminded moms and professionals who can bring you through an incredible transformation—mind, body, and soul. Continue this journey with us, and join our *Balance for Busy Moms* Tribe for lifelong positive changes. Make your life the best you've ever dreamed of with your spouse and children. The heart matters. You matter. Learn to build a force field of love around you and your children. Learn to raise your vibration and create the most positive outcome of any circumstance. Gain the knowledge and learn the proper tools for creating the changes necessary to prevent illness and overcome stress and adversity. Learn to properly guide your children with love, improve your home, and heal your relationships with self-compassion and service. Unite with community. Learn about branding and following your dreams for a fulfilling career and service to our planet.

Join our *Balance for Busy Moms* Tribe for unlimited access to ongoing health and wellness classes, taught by experienced professionals— our co-authors, who have the secrets, keys, and strategies for mom's success. Develop lasting friendships with other moms, start threads on important matters, download workouts, recipes, cleanses and detox methods, receive a free *Balance for Busy Moms* book as a giveaway, and more surprises and monthly bonuses.

Just visit www.balanceforbusymomstribe.com and get started with us today!

CPSIA information can be obtained at www.ICGtesting.com
Printed in the USA
BVOW11s1112160314

347797BV00003B/22/P